YORK NOTES

General Editors: Professor A.N. Jeffares (*University of Stirling*) & Professor Suheil Bushrui (*American University of Beirut*)

Seamus Heaney

SELECTED POEMS

Notes by Aisling Maguire
BA PH D (N U I)

LONGMAN
YORK PRESS

YORK PRESS
Immeuble Esseily, Place Riad Solh, Beirut.

LONGMAN GROUP UK LIMITED
Longman House, Burnt Mill, Harlow,
Essex CM20 2JE, England
Associated companies, branches and representatives
throughout the world

First published 1986
Sixth impression 1991

ISBN 0-582-02306-8

Produced by Longman Group (FE) Ltd.
Printed in Hong Kong

Contents

Part 1

Introduction

The life of Seamus Heaney

Seamus Heaney was born on 13 April 1939, the eldest in a family of nine children. The family home was a farm at Bellaghy in the south of County Derry in Northern Ireland. The Heaneys trace their local origins to a twelfth-century saint, Muredach O'Heney, founder of a church in the northern part of the county. Both Seamus Heaney's father and grandfather were farmers, and it was expected that he would follow in this tradition.

The countryside that surrounds Bellaghy is rich in historical associations. Mild and fertile farmland rises on one side to cover the low slopes of Slieve Gallion and gives way on the other side to the dark expanse of a bog or moss. Opposite the bog lies Lough Beg and in the middle of this lake is Church Island, believed to have been a place of prayer and fasting visited by St Patrick.

Religious history is overwritten by the history of English colonisation. Place names such as Castledawson, Grove Hill and the Demesne are reminders of the period when Ulster was settled by Scottish and English landowners. Although the resulting divisions persist within Northern Irish society the farming community at Bellaghy was bound together by its common needs.

During the Second World War (1939–45) in Europe Northern Ireland was designated as a US naval and airforce base. Four air raids struck Belfast but there was little direct enemy action in rural areas. Seamus Heaney recalls the food rationing, the radio bulletins from Europe, and, occasionally, an American plane seen overhead. At Anahorish the schoolhouse was requisitioned for an aerodrome and classes were held instead in a Nissen hut. Here Heaney learnt to recite passages from the works of Byron and Keats.

Winning a scholarship at the age of twelve he was sent away as a boarder to St Columb's College in the city of Derry. Another scholarship enabled him to go from school to Queen's University in Belfast where he read for an honours degree in English.

The urge to write poetry was not strongly felt by Seamus Heaney during his years at university. A handful of poems by him appeared in the college magazine, *Gorgon*, some of them printed over the reticent pen-name, 'incertus'. With the arrival in Belfast of the English critic, Philip

Hobsbaum, a new impetus was given to those with a serious interest in writing. Every Monday evening young poets would gather at the Hobsbaums' house to read and discuss one another's work. The 'group', as they came to be known, included Michael and Edna Longley, James Simmons, Stewart Parker, Seamus Deane (a schoolfriend of Seamus Heaney) and Marie Devlin (to whom Heaney is now married).

On leaving Queen's University with a first class BA degree Seamus Heaney took up the post of English teacher at St Joseph's Technical College, Belfast. He continued to attend the weekly poetry meetings and began to have work published in various Irish newspapers and journals. When the Hobsbaums left Belfast in 1965, the reputation, both collective and individual, of the Group had spread to London and Dublin. In an article written in 1963 Seamus Heaney has referred to this resurgence of cultural activity in Belfast and pointed out the need in the North of Ireland for a good literary magazine:

> It could perform a useful service in the Northern community—the artist is the custodian of human values, of sanity and tolerance and these are the qualities most needed in the North of today.

Already his conviction about the significance of the poet in society had taken shape. For a time he continued to hold the poetry evenings in his flat but gradually the circle dispersed, its members moving to jobs outside Belfast.

In 1966 Seamus Heaney's first collection of poems, *Death of a Naturalist*, was published by Faber and Faber. By now he had been appointed to a lectureship in the English Department at Queen's University, and at this time he married Marie Devlin. The next six years were productive ones. Heaney contributed articles and book reviews to the *Listener* and in 1969 his second collection *Door into the Dark*, was published. He spent the academic year of 1970/1 on a sabbatical at Berkeley University, California. Here he came in contact with the poets Gary Snyder and Robert Bly, whose free-verse techniques had some influence on his own writing. He also saw at this time the emergence of the ethnic revival in America, a movement that introduced a new appreciation of the patterns of folklore and primitive traditions and handcrafts. Some of the poems in his next volume, *Wintering Out*, published in 1972, reflect the influence of these American poets.

As the violence that had broken out in the North of Ireland in 1969 continued, Seamus Heaney became aware of a new pressure being exerted on him as a poet. With three collections now to his credit he had become a public figure. There was less and less time for him to be alone and to write. It was expected, too, that, as an established poet, he should turn his literary skills to a political end and voice the cause of the nationalist minority. These factors, coupled with the physical strain of living in such an unnatural atmosphere, contributed to his decision to leave Belfast.

Determined to become a full-time writer, he resigned his post at Queen's University. He and his family left Belfast in 1973, on being offered the use of a friend's cottage, Glanmore Cottage (a back-gate lodge on the former Synge estate, Glanmore Castle) at Ashford, County Wicklow, in the Republic of Ireland. Wicklow is renowned for the richness and variety of its scenery. Here Heaney was reminded of his native South Derry landscape and set to work on the translation of a medieval Irish poem, *Buile Shuibhne Geilt* (literally *The Lament of Mad Sweaney*; Heaney's title is *Sweeney Astray*), long passages of which express a lyrical delight in nature.

During this time in Wicklow Heaney completed the poems for his fourth collection, *North* (1975) and continued to write essays and reviews for various Irish and English periodicals. After three years of rural calm the Heaney family moved to Dublin, where he was appointed head of the English department at Carysfort Teacher Training College. In 1982 he was invited to be Poet in Residence at Harvard University in Boston, Massachusetts. The stipulation of his five-year contract here was that he should spend four months of each academic year on campus. The syllabus Heaney drew up for his classes concentrated on contemporary writers, including the work of Central and Eastern European poets.

So, over a decade after his departure from Belfast, Seamus Heaney is once again a public figure. He is generous with his time, giving regular readings and interviews on radio and television. Although he is willing to speak about his work to journalists in every area of the media, both academic and general, he is anxious at the same time to preserve its mystery. His personable manner and the human quality of his poetry have given Heaney and his work a wide popular appeal.

The significance of this public persona is enhanced by Heaney's belief in the active role of a poet and in the power of poetic truth within a community. Thus the altruism of the communal spirit that surrounded him as a child in Bellaghy has remained a constant value in his life and poetry.

The work of Seamus Heaney

Seamus Heaney has published six major collections of verse, one small volume of prose poems, a selection of prose and a translation from a Middle Irish poem. Limited editions have been printed of certain poem sequences such as 'A Lough Neagh Sequence' from *Door into the Dark*. His work is widely represented in anthologies and some of it has been translated into Polish and Hungarian among other languages.

His work follows an autobiographical narrative shape. From the first poems, written from the point of view of a child, he passes through a period of self-doubt to reach the uneasy reflections of middle age. As a critic he brings an informed intuition to bear on the work of other poets. He invariably concentrates on the active quality of the words in a poem and the features emphasised in his criticism correspond to those stressed in his poetry.

Preoccupations: Selected Prose 1968–1978 takes its title from an essay by W.B. Yeats in which he states that ' . . . the following of art is little different from the following of religion in the intense preoccupation it demands.'* The essays in this volume fall into three categories: incidental reminiscences commissioned for journals and broadcasts; lectures on the work of other poets and a selection of book reviews. In each of these articles Heaney is concerned with the relationship between the poet's environment and the development of his imagination. Commitment to poetry he understands as a commitment to language. He listens for the sound of the poet's speaking voice.

Gerard Manley Hopkins (1844–89) was the first poet to inspire in Heaney the desire to write poetry.† In the energetic language of the English poet he sensed a similarity with the dialect of his own region. The poems written during his years at university bear the signs of this apprenticeship, with a heavy use of alliteration and word-pairs such as 'thatch-watches' and 'dust-drunk'. After university he took his cue from the works of the Irish poet Patrick Kavanagh (1904–67), the English poet Ted Hughes (*b.* 1930), now the Poet Laureate, and the Welsh poet R.S. Thomas (*b.* 1913). His early poetry, written under the influence of their rural naturalism, demonstrates his awareness of the literary potential of his own background.

Farm work and farmyard scenes perceived by the small boy are described with the hindsight of the man in *Death of a Naturalist*. Death is evident in various forms, the seasonal process of decay as in 'Blackberry Picking', the death of his younger brother in 'Mid-Term Break', and the passing of innocence in the title poem. Throughout the collection a subversive energy threatens the stability of the boy's environment. Even later, as a lover, he remains wary.

Door into the Dark proceeds directly from the concluding poem of the previous collection and undertakes a ritual invocation of the unseen energy that governs life and death. At the centre of the collection 'A Lough Neagh Sequence' draws on the lore of the eel-fishers at Ardboe

* *Preoccupations*, Faber and Faber, London, 1980, epigraph.
† A convert to Catholicism who later became a Jesuit priest, he is renowned for his baroque diction and for his invention of 'sprung rhythm'. From 1884 until his death in 1889 he was Professor of Greek at University College, Dublin (then part of the Royal University of Ireland).

in County Tyrone. In *Wintering Out* the mystery is equated with the source of language. A number of place-name poems in the old Irish tradition of 'Dinnseanchas' (place-name poems) trace geographical details in the spelling and pronunciation of the name. Many of the poems here have an allegorical form touching on the origins of the social division which had once again provoked violent conflict in the North of Ireland.

By a coincidence, in 1969, the year when this conflict began, a book entitled *The Bog People: Iron Age Man Preserved* by P.V. Glob, a Danish archaeologist, was published.* The book documents the discovery of Iron Age bodies in European bogs, especially in Denmark and Ireland. Professor Glob concludes that these are the bodies of victims sacrificed to appease a primitive goddess of fertility. On his seeing some of the photographs from the text reproduced elsewhere Seamus Heaney's imagination was stirred. The bog which had been a part of the poet's childhood world now acquired a new significance. A later reading of *The Bog People* provided him with the focus for a series of poems published in a limited edition as *Bog Poems* and subsequently included in *North*.

Having explored his Gaelic past in *Wintering Out* the poet turns in this new sequence to the Norse strain in his heritage. The bodies of the ancient sacrificial victims are juxtaposed with the victims of the continuing battle in the North of Ireland. They provide a physical key to the darkness probed in his previous collections. Their preservation in the bog is seen by Heaney to correspond to the survival of certain Norse words in his dialect.

The chief development represented by *Field Work*, Heaney's fifth collection, is the use of metre. The sonnets and elegies are allusive as the poet calls up the shades and voices of literary predecessors from Shakespeare and Dante to Wordsworth, Yeats and Robert Lowell. The formal arrangements of metre and diction are subverted by Heaney's dialect. In the same way the poet himself is disturbed by visions, dreams and ghosts whom he questions and by whom he wants to be questioned.

Station Island, his most recent work, continues this process as the poet on a pilgrimage encounters the shades of friends and of the Irish writers William Carleton (1794–1869), Patrick Kavanagh and James Joyce (1882–1941). Through all of these voices he disputes the merit and direction of his own poetry.

For ten years Seamus Heaney worked on his translation of *Buile Shuibhne Geilt* which he has rendered as *Sweeney Astray*. The story

* P.V. Glob, *The Bog People: Iron Age Man Preserved*, Faber and Faber, London, 1969.

told in this poem concerns a legendary king of Ulster who, punished by a Christian cleric for blasphemy, is condemned to live the life of a bird. From the moment that he is cursed Sweeney's narrative alternates between delight in his natural surroundings and self-pity for the physical discomforts he suffers. His state of mind reflects the conflict between the old pagan modes of belief and the new Christian doctrine. Even as he dies in the arms of a monk he refuses to renounce his pagan ideas.

Heaney detects in Sweeney's uneasy consciousness a parallel with the isolated figure of the past. He writes that ' . . . it is possible to read the work as an aspect of the quarrel between free creative imagination and the constraints of religious, political and domestic obligation'.* Sweeney is the fullest expression of a divided sensibility that underpins Seamus Heaney's work. It was present in his youthful mingled fear of, and fascination with, the natural processes and later it manifested itself in the crossed Celtic and Norse strains of the poet's ancestry. The uncertainty of the poet's response to the bog bodies and to those killed in his own society continues this theme. Sweeney, the legendary figure, half bird and half man, provides a retrospective understanding of the foundation and progress of Seamus Heaney's poetry.

Historical background

That part of Northern Ireland ruled today by the English government at Westminster is a product of the complex links that have bound Ireland to England since the twelfth century.

Rivalries and conflicts between the tribal kingdoms within Ireland facilitated its colonisation by England. The first settlers were Anglo-Normans. They held land in the environs of Dublin on the east coast, an area that later became known as the Pale. They owed allegiance to the King of England.

During the reign of the Tudor monarchs fear of a rebellion in Ireland, supported by Spain, the leading Catholic power on the Continent, (which landed troops in Ireland) forced the English to extend their power throughout Ireland. After Henry VIII's break with the Pope in Rome England had become Protestant and the Anglican Church (with Henry at its head) became the Established Church of England.

As Ireland became more English in customs and government the Earls of Ulster†(the northern Kingdom) rose against the forces of the English Crown. Lack of equipment and a delay in the arrival of help from Spain contributed to their defeat. Their surrender coincided with

---

* *Sweeney Astray*, Field Day, Derry, 1983, p.viii.
† Hugh O'Neill, Earl of Tyrone, and Hugh Roe O'Donnell, Earl of Tyrconnel.

the death of Queen Elizabeth I.* The Earls then fled to Europe hoping to find there more support for their cause.

On the accession of James I to the English throne, Ulster was the province that most threatened the security of the crown in Ireland. The large estates of the Earls were seized and plans were made to settle them with loyal subjects from England. The claims of the Crown were pressed to the utmost and six of the nine Ulster counties—Armagh, Cavan, Coleraine (later renamed Londonderry), Donegal, Fermanagh, Tyrone —were declared to be in the King's hands and open to colonisation. A small area within each one was to be reserved for the native Irish.

Scottish and English settlers were brought over. They laid out farms and built small fortified buildings or enclosures known as 'bawns'. The settlers adapted well to life in Ulster and brought a new prosperity to the province by setting up small industries in their towns. The Scots had brought with them, too, their own form of protestantism, the Presbyterian church. Later attempts by the English government to impose conformity on the Irish and Anglo-Norman Catholics were extended to the Scottish Presbyterians who had initially settled in County Antrim.

From this time onward English relations with Ireland were dictated by two factors: one, in order to maintain authority in Ireland the English government had to appoint English administrators and needed to keep a standing army in Ireland; two, the cost of both these institutions was high and the 'plantations' provided a source of revenue and loyalty.

The history of Ulster was decided by the Battle of the Boyne in 1690. The power of the Roman Catholics in Europe, backed by the Spanish Empire and the Papal See, made the presence of Catholics in Ireland a significant threat to the English throne. The settlement of Ulster had not fully secured the loyalty of that area, for the Presbyterians there were in sympathy with their Scottish co-religionists who sought to establish and spread the authority of their church. A greater number of the native Irish had remained in Ulster than had been allowed for in the original plans.

In 1641 an insurrection broke out in Ulster. The native Irish Catholics sought, with the support of the Old English (Anglo-Norman) Catholics in the Pale, to gain control of the province and secure a guarantee of religious liberty from the government. The following year the two groups formed a Confederation, its aim being to establish a separate system of

* According to J.C. Beckett, *The Making of Modern Ireland 1603–1923*, Faber and Faber, London, 1966; rev. edn. 1981, vol. 1, p.23, the Earls made 'abject submission' to Queen Elizabeth, and her representative, Mountjoy, on 30 March 1602. They were unaware at the time that the Queen had died. By the treaty that followed this surrender the Irish Earls subordinated their power to that of the English monarch. This marked the end of an independent Gaelic society and resulted in concerted opposition to English rule.

government. Their interests, however, were not entirely compatible. Much of the land owned by the native Irish had been confiscated by the Crown, while the Old English continued to hold large estates. The longer the war continued the greater would be their loss. This internal division and a lack of military equipment and expertise weakened their strength. The war lasted for ten years and ended with the arrival of Oliver Cromwell.

The war in Ireland was an extension of English dissatisfaction with the reign of Charles I. His refusal to grant authority to the Parliament and his extravagance with state money had caused a rift between the King and the Parliament. In the battles that ensued Oliver Cromwell led the army of the Parliament to victory over that of the King. The King was captured and subsequently executed.

A military genius and a zealous puritan, Oliver Cromwell has become a legendary figure in Irish history with many apocryphal tales attached to his name. For Cromwell the nine-month campaign in Ireland was a crusade. He was determined to quell the Catholic rebellion and establish a Protestant state. After his first engagement in Ireland, the siege of Drogheda (a strategic coastal town thirty miles north of Dublin) in which three thousand people died and all the members of the Catholic clergy were put to death, his reputation verged on the demonic. Most of the other towns surrendered at his approach but another fierce siege at Wexford on the south-east coast added to his notoriety. On his return to England Cromwell quickly arrogated power and, in 1653, proclaimed himself Lord Protector of England, Scotland and Ireland.

During the seventeenth century gifts of Irish land were made as payment to Englishmen who had supported the cause of Oliver Cromwell. A policy of conversion to Puritanism was pursued without success by his Commonwealth government. Under King Charles II, however, a period of stability and prosperity followed and the linen industry expanded. Catholics in Ireland were tolerated until the discovery of a Catholic plot to overthrow the King forced him to adopt a more oppressive policy.

His successor, James II, reversed this oppressive policy, appointing an Irish Earl, Tyrconnel, a Catholic, to the position of Lord Lieutenant (the King's representative in Ireland). Despite promises that the settlement of land would remain as it was the Protestant settlers were disturbed. They grew anxious for their financial security and many of them returned to England. After Tyrconnel dismissed all Protestants from the army, English Protestant opposition to King James mounted rapidly. In a show of support for the King, Tyrconnel despatched some of his troops to England, a move which weakened his garrisons in Ulster and exacerbated Protestant fears.

The soldiers dismissed from the army sought the help of William of Orange in Holland (James II's son-in-law). In order to supply James II with troops to display his power in England the Earl of Tyrconnel now withdrew the garrison from the town of Londonderry in Ulster.

The arrival of King William in England precipitated the Irish Protestants into action, and the citizens of Londonderry enclosed themselves within their town to resist the arrival of a new garrison. Their success inspired other Protestants in Ulster who set about forming defensive associations. When William was declared King of England the Irish Protestants adopted him as their leader too.

The confrontation between the two kings vying for power in England in 1690 took place at the river Boyne in Ireland, with troops of mixed nationality on both sides. James was supported by English, Irish and French soldiers, while William had Dutch, German, English and Irish troops on his side. The battle had a European significance, but for Ireland it represented the overthrow of the Catholic nobility. Most of these nobles were descended from the first Anglo-Norman settlers, and some were native Irish who had accepted honours from the English crown. As a group, they had survived the plantations under both Elizabeth and Cromwell. In 1641 fifty-nine per cent of the land was owned by them but by 1703 only fourteen per cent was still in their hands. The new English owners preferred to remain in England leaving their property in the care of stewards who rented it to local farmers. High rents and poor living conditions caused much social unrest.

After the defeat of King James at the river Boyne power was vested in the Protestant ascendancy. The Irish parliament, now reconstituted, survived until the end of the eighteenth century. This parliament gave the Irish Protestants the power they needed to legislate to their own advantage. The wool and linen industries were controlled by them but they were afraid that the English government might impose trade restrictions in order to protect English industry.

This fear was realised in 1699 when the parliament prohibited the export of woollen goods to any country other than England. A high tariff on these imports prevented their sale in England. In the eyes of the Protestants in Ireland such measures negated the independent status of their parliament, and as a result of these restrictions a nationalist spirit arose among them. Another source of anxiety to them was the growing power of the Ulster Presbyterians whose commercial success was evident in the towns of Londonderry and Belfast.

Half of the population of Ulster was Protestant. Protestants were to be found in every class of society, being landowners, merchants, and factory workers and farm labourers, while the Catholics were predominantly farm labourers and tenant farmers. These tenants on farms were better off in Ulster than elsewhere in Ireland. A 'custom' prevailed assuring their right to sell or exchange land. Emigration to America after a rent rise resulted in a better distribution of land. At this time a distinctive middle-class population began to emerge in Ulster consisting of tradesmen, merchants and small landowners, all of whom were Protestant. Out of a population of ten thousand in Belfast in 1708 only seven were Roman Catholics.

Catholics throughout Ireland were now persecuted by a system of 'penal laws' which denied them the right to vote or to own land. Revolutionary sentiments filtered through to Ireland after the American War of Independence (1775−83) and the French Revolution which began in 1789. A common desire for independence from the English Crown drew together the Irish Catholics and Presbyterians and some Protestants. Bands of volunteers, originally formed as a protection against a possible French invasion, were now joined by men who professed revolutionary ideals. Many Presbyterians began to agitate for the reform of the penal laws. A committee set up in Dublin to press for these reforms elected a Protestant barrister to be its chairman.

The aim of this man, Theobald Wolfe Tone (1763−98), was to unite all Irishmen and to establish religious equality. Joining with the Ulster Presbyterians he formed a group called the United Irishmen. In Ulster, however, rivalry had broken out between the Protestant and Catholic tenants. A rise in population had caused competition for land and this frequently led to conflict. After a pitched battle in Armagh in 1795 the victorious Protestants formed the Orange Society. The declared intention of this Society was to maintain Protestant ascendancy over the Catholic population.

Wolfe Tone turned to France for support for a rebellion. Landlords raised a force of yeomen to protect their estates. In Ulster the United Irishmen had set up a military organisation. Peasants were armed with muskets and pikes. Belfast was the centre of this revolutionary action, the small number of people involved enjoying a wide popular support. The government sent in the yeomen and the militia to prevent an uprising. This reduced the support for a revolution and the simultaneous rise of a new evangelical movement further pacified the Ulster Protestants.

Between 1797 and 1798 chaos spread through Ireland. Revolutionary fervour continued to be strong in the west and south. Although most of the leaders had been arrested, an insurrection was staged in May 1798. The original plan was not followed and the insurrection disintegrated into sporadic risings in different areas. The final confrontation took place at Vinegar Hill, outside Enniscorthy in County Wexford. Gathered at a local camp, the rebels who had attempted to set up their own government were surrounded and twenty thousand of them killed.

The resulting instability in the country encouraged support for a proposal of legislative Union joining the English and the Irish governments. Although it was promised that religious emancipation would follow the Union the proposal was opposed by Catholics. Likewise, the Orange Society which had expanded and begun to revive animosity between Catholic and Protestant labourers, was opposed to the Union. As the events taking place in France under the new regime became known the revolutionary ardour of the Ulster Presbyterians abated and they too supported the proposed Union. Support for the Union was increased by fears of a French invasion, an event that would require the assistance of the English army.

In 1800 a bill establishing 'The United Kingdom of Great Britain and Ireland' was passed in the Irish House of Lords. Resigned to their defeat, some of those who had opposed the Union now accepted positions in the Irish executive; others, particularly the landlords, moved to London and left their estates in the charge of agents. This was to lead to trouble in the future.

Social and economic differences between Ulster and the rest of Ireland were accentuated in the nineteenth century. The linen industry had now surpassed the English one. Spinning and weaving were home-based industries providing a livelihood for many families who owned small areas of land.

In 1845 Ireland was one of the most densely populated countries in Europe. Four-fifths of its eight million inhabitants lived by the land and half the population depended on the potato crop as its only source of food. The failure of the entire potato crop for three successive years caused famine throughout the country.

Government policy maintained that Irish poverty should be alleviated by the Irish propertied class. Disease spread and such medical services as existed were inadequate to the scale of the epidemic. Between 1845 and 1850 a million people died. About the same number or more emigrated, the majority going to the United States and to British North America (Canada). Many died in transit on the crowded ships.

By the beginning of the twentieth century the Irish population had been reduced by half. The basis of Irish politics and Irish society was profoundly altered in this period. How best to improve Irish agriculture and remedy the grievances between tenant and landlord dominated Anglo-Irish relations for the fifty years subsequent to the famine.

Farming methods in Ulster changed from tillage to pasture. As the manufacturing industries grew, unemployed farm labourers found work in the cities. Engineering and ship-building industries now developed in Belfast. In the 1860s this city became one of the major industrial centres in England and Ireland.

A parliamentary party dedicated to 'Home Rule' emerged at this period. It sought limited autonomy within a federal system, while retaining loyalty to the Crown. Popular support for the party was based on a nationalistic belief in the Irish right to self-government. Despite the fact that the Irish Parliamentary Party was led by a Protestant landowner, Charles Stewart Parnell (1846–91), it won the votes of the Catholic clergy.

The commitment of the Liberal Prime Minister of England, William Gladstone (1809–98), to Home Rule caused unease among Irish Protestants. For them it signalled the end to the right of the Protestant ascendancy to rule in Ireland. Besides, they enjoyed economic benefits from the union and had access to good positions in the army and the public service. An Irish government in Ireland would, they knew, be a predominantly Catholic one. Opposition was strongest in Ulster where Protestants controlled most of the wealth. Rivalry between Catholics and Protestants for land and employment persisted.

A Dublin government would result in the decline of the prosperity of the Ulster Protestants. Once again the Orange Order (formerly the Orange Society) provided a structure for their common insecurity. They were willing to accept any agreement that guaranteed a special position to their province. The Conservative party adopted their case and opposed Home Rule. As Home Rule bills were tabled in parliament in 1886, 1893 and 1912 sectarian rioting broke out in Ulster. In 1895 an Ulster Defence Union was formed to resist the government. Although the notion of a separate Ulster interest had taken hold, the policy of this Union was founded in the interest of all Ireland.

At the beginning of the twentieth century a new nationalist movement, inspired by a nineteenth-century romantic interest in the past, had spread through Europe. A corresponding movement in Ireland was begun through the medium of the English language. The Irish literary revival was started by a group of Anglo-Irish intellectuals including Lady Gregory (1852–1932), W.B. Yeats (1865–1939), George Russell (A.E., 1867–1935), and Douglas Hyde (1860–1949). This last writer straddled the linguistic divide and was instrumental in the founding of the Gaelic League in 1893 for the promotion of Irish as a spoken language. His collection of translations of Irish poems, *Lovesongs of Connaught*, was much admired by Yeats.

The intention of these writers was to create a body of work in English that would be distinctively Irish, taking its subjects from Celtic mythology and folklore. When J.M. Synge (1871–1909) joined the group he introduced a unique rhythmical idiom based on country dialects and accents.

In 1897–8 the Irish Literary Theatre was formed and the Abbey Theatre (still the Irish National Theatre) was founded in 1904. Within all of these groups and societies were people dedicated to the ideal of an

Irish Ireland and some of them were determined to achieve this by revolutionary means.

As negotiations for a Home Rule Bill advanced, the Ulster Unionists began to train a military force known as the Ulster Volunteers. Their statement of policy was sanctioned by Protestant bishops and ministers. Although they declared their loyalty to the Crown, they were prepared to rebel against the constitutional authority. A member of the Liberal party suggested that a provision be made in the Home Rule Bill to exclude Ulster from its conditions. This was rejected by the party but opinion was divided and the proposal was raised in subsequent debates.

At the outbreak of war in Europe in 1914 the leaders of the Irish Parliamentary Party and of the unionists agreed to allow the Home Rule Bill proposed by Lord Asquith to be passed but its enactment to be suspended until after the war. On the basis of this agreement John Redmond and Edward Carson pledged the support of their parties to the English government for the duration of the war. Many Irishmen fought in the British forces, in the trenches of France and Belgium and many were killed at Gallipoli.

An Irish Volunteer force had been formed, similar to the Ulster Volunteers, in order to display the determination of the nationalists to control their own future, in the same way as the unionists had done by forming their own Volunteer force. Its founders declared that it was to be 'protective and defensive' but members of the subversive Irish Republican Brotherhood quickly infiltrated its ranks. In 1916 this group planned a rising to take place under cover of Volunteer manoeuvres. The plan was discovered at the last hour by the head of the Volunteers, and the risings were stopped everywhere except in Dublin. There, strategic buildings were seized during Easter week. The proclamation of an Irish Republic was read outside the General Post Office. A week later the rebels had surrendered. The subsequent execution of the leaders of this rising aroused public sympathy for their cause.

Other leaders released from jail established a nationalist party. They reaffirmed the declaration of independence and set up an alternative government of Ireland in 1919. Civil war directed against the supporters of the Crown ensued in 1920. The new Irish parliament professed to rule Ulster too and this aroused the resentment of the Ulster Unionists. Sectarian riots continued throughout 1920 in Belfast. The government in England was unable to protect the nationalists in Ulster and the unionists in the south.

A Government of Ireland Act was signed in 1920. The north and south were to have their own parliaments and the supremacy of the imperial parliament was to be retained. This partition of Ireland was not intended to be permanent or complete.

The republicans opposed the Act and entered into discussions with the government. A year later an Anglo-Irish treaty was signed. Ireland was to be a dominion. Members of the Irish Parliament were to swear allegiance to the Crown. If the people of Northern Ireland wished they could be excluded from this Free State and retain the status accorded to them under the Government of Ireland Act. The boundary between north and south was to be redefined. When this border was drawn towns and farms were divided in order to ensure a Unionist majority within the six counties that had chosen to remain separate from the Irish Free State. Political constituencies within the six counties were designed on a similar principle. Today there are approximately one million unionists and six hundred thousand nationalists in Northern Ireland.

In 1932 the Free State of Ireland repudiated its allegiance to the English Crown and declared itself a republic. The old unionist fears of economic rivalry with the nationalists resulted in an active policy of discrimination against the nationalists in Northern Ireland. Opportunities for employment and housing were denied them, thereby restricting their power to vote and achieve representation in the government of Northern Ireland. A growing mood of dissatisfaction among Catholic nationalists found expression in a protest march by the Civil Rights Association in October 1968. The R.U.C. (the Royal Ulster Constabulary) batoned some of the protesters, an incident which precipitated the present conflict in Northern Ireland.

A note on the text

Seamus Heaney's *Selected Poems 1965–1975* was published in London by Faber and Faber in 1980. It is divided into four sections corresponding to Heaney's first four collections: *Death of a Naturalist*, *Door into the Dark*, *Wintering Out* and *North*. There is a logical coherence to the selection which bears out the poet's view of these works as comprising a single book that 'grows together and goes together'.*

The only alterations to the original poems are made in the length of the poem sequences. 'Setting', Part 4 of 'A Lough Neagh Sequence' from *Door into the Dark*, is reduced from six verses to three. Parts 2 and 4 of 'A Northern Hoard' in *Wintering Out* are omitted, as are Parts 3 and 4 of 'Singing School' in *North*. The division of *North* into two parts is not adopted in the *Selected Poems*, and *North*, Part II, is represented only by 'Singing School'. An epigraph to the title of this poem with quotations from William Wordsworth (1770–1850) and W.B. Yeats is not included.

---

* J. Haffenden, *Viewpoints: Poets in Conversation*, Faber and Faber, London, 1981, p.64.

In making this selection the poet has been careful to choose poems from the various collections that are compatible. Many of those excluded deal with love, marriage and pregnancy, others are descriptions of other artists, painters, writers and singers.

Part 2

Summaries
of SELECTED POEMS

THE WORD 'GROWTH' is repeated by Seamus Heaney in descriptions of his own work, implying that he regards his poetic development as an organic process. Through the works represented in the *Selected Poems 1965–1975* there is a noticeable concentration of the poet's focus as he pursues particular themes first raised in his early poems. Set in the region where he grew up, these works have an autobiographical shape.

The fears of the child in *Death of a Naturalist* are magnified into the awe of the man in *North*. Heaney's early fascination with the sound and movement of words eventually makes language itself the subject of his poetry. The historical division that undermines the society in which he lives gives way to another inner division as the poet recognises the primitive aspects of his own human nature. These developments are expressed in the voices of the different personae that move through the works from the curious boy to the anxious poet.

'Digging'   *Death of a Naturalist*

Three generations of the poet's family are depicted in this poem. The poet sits writing, his hand wrapped around his pen as though it were a gun. The sound of his father digging comes to him through the window. Looking out he can see his father turning soil in the flower-beds and remembers how as children he and his brothers and sisters had helped their father to lift the potatoes.

His father's skill at digging matches that of his father, the poet's grandfather. Now the poet recalls bringing milk to his grandfather as he worked on the bog. The old man stopped only long enough to drink and went back to his task.

The smell of the potatoes and the noise of the turf as it was dug return to the poet and with them he becomes aware of a vital link that binds him to his family. Despite this bond the poet rejects the family tradition, saying that he does not have the same skills as his forbears. Instead, he resolves to dig with the pen which lies now in his hand like a spade.

COMMENTARY: Of this poem Seamus Heaney has said that it was his first 'real' poem:

This was the first place where I felt I had done more than make an arrangement of words: I felt I had let down a shaft into real life.*

Apart from the three generations of his family described here the three main areas of the poet's life are defined, the political, the private and the traditional. He is caught in the recurrent dilemma of the artist wanting both to act and to create.

Two paths of action are open to him, represented by the gun and the spade. Although the poem was written in 1964, five years before the outbreak of the present violence in the North of Ireland, the people of that region were brought up with an awareness of a history in which sectarian conflict was frequent. The neat balance of the opening couplet is disturbed in the final verse by the removal of the phrase 'snug as a gun'. To an extent this imbalance is redressed by the new third line. The original alternative weighed by the poet is replaced by the association of the pen and the spade.

The free structure imitates the reflective mood of the poet as his comments intervene between the descriptive passages. His memories impinge on each of his five senses. The scenes of his father and grandfather digging are brought to life by the 'clean rasping sound' of the spade and by the sight of his father in the flower-bed; the poet recalls the 'cool hardness' of the potatoes and the smell of the 'potato mould'. These sensations are reproduced by the concrete vocabulary and its patterns of sound:

> The cold smell of potato mould, the squelch and slap
> Of soggy peat, the curt cuts of an edge
> Through living roots awaken in my head.

The poet uses his pen with the same facility as his father does the spade.

In the fourth verse the automatic ease of the farmer's movement is conveyed by the word 'nestled', its suggestion of comfort matching that of 'snug' in the first verse. Certain sounds repeated through the fourth verse emphasise the 'rhythm' of the digging as 'boot' is echoed in 'rooted' and 'cool'. In the second last verse 'roots' picks up this sequence of sound and underlines the poet's refusal to follow his father. The roots he refers to are not the solid ones of the potato plant.

The poet's diction is relaxed and conversational, as he uses the contractions 'I've' and 'I'll' and colloquial phrases such as 'fell to', used of someone settling straightaway to work. The two lines of the fifth verse are interjected like a spoken voice:

> By God, the old man could handle a spade.
> Just like his old man.

* 'Feeling into Words', *Preoccupations: Selected Prose 1968-1978*, Faber and Faber, London, 1980, p.8.

Introduced by the emphatic exclamation 'By God' they ring with the abrupt idiom of the poet's district.

The farmyard provides the location for many of Heaney's early poems but lurking beneath its ordered routines is the loaded danger of the gun.

NOTES AND GLOSSARY:

turf:	cut from the dry top layer of a bog; it contains the roots and grass that grow on the surface
bog:	marshy ground formed by compressed vegetable matter and sphagnum moss. Sods of this matter when cut and dried are used as fuel in Ireland (and other countries, notably Denmark). The centre of Ireland is covered by large tracts of bogland
peat:	cut from within the bog and a brown colour, it is used for fuel

'Death of a Naturalist'   *Death of a Naturalist*

Here the poet casts himself as a young boy. The poem opens with an evocation of the summer humidity rising from a flax-dam. The child watches the stagnant water and names the insects that hover above it. He collects frogspawn to keep in jars so that he can see the tadpoles hatching. At school the teacher explains the process to the children in simple terms. She adds the information that frogs indicate the weather by the colour of their backs.

Again the boy goes out to the flax-dam but now he finds that it has been taken over by large bullfrogs. The smell in the fields is stronger and the noise from the dam is louder than before. Suddenly he feels threatened by the croaking of the frogs and imagines that if he puts his hand into the water it will be trapped by the spawn. This, he thinks, will be the frogs' revenge on him for stealing their offspring. Sickened by fear he runs away from the dam.

COMMENTARY: As in 'Digging' the familiar world of the poet is menaced by a force defined in terms of weapons: the frogs become 'mud grenades'. A mildly ironic tone is introduced by the title and the poet takes an amused look at his childish fears. He repeats the teacher's simplistic phrases: the 'mammy frog' and the 'daddy frog', her condescending attitude taking no account of the child's intensity of feeling.

His unquestioning sensual pleasure in natural life is violated by his new knowledge. In the first part of the poem the rotting flax-dam is concealed by the 'delicate' noise of the bubbles. The sound of the insects acts like a bandage, a 'strong gauze', containing the spread of decay. Frogspawn appeals to the child like cream and jam, its substance 'clotted' and 'jellied'. The sounds change in the second part becoming crude and ugly: 'croaking'; 'slap'; 'plop'; 'farting'. 'Gross-bellied' frogs replace the 'jellied' spawn.

Patterns of imitative words create the dense physical atmosphere of this poem:

> There were dragon-flies, spotted butterflies,
> But best of all was the warm thick slobber
> Of frogspawn that grew like clotted water

The sound of the onomatopoeic word 'slobber' is amplified by the internal rhyme of 'spotted' and 'clotted' and the short 'o's of 'dragon' and 'frog'. The end-rhyme too of 'slobber' and 'water' supplements the effect, particularly as the rhymes in this poem are, for the most part, internal. In the phrase 'But best of all' the child's natural speaking voice is heard.

You should trace the further echoes of these sounds within the poem and notice how their altered effect corresponds to the change that comes over the child.

NOTES AND GLOSSARY:

flax dam: bank where the harvested flax is left to dry before being processed to make linen

---

'At a Potato Digging' *Death of a Naturalist*

This four-part sequence opens on a scene of people gathering potatoes. The vegetables are uprooted by a machine and the gatherers collect them in baskets. The fingers of the workers are numb with the cold.

Moving in uneven lines they resemble a flock of crows and the ground is dark as the plumage of a crow. They work in twos, carrying the full baskets between them to be emptied into a pit. Bent over the soil they look like fishermen hauling a catch from the sea. The labourers respect the land because they depend on it to sustain them.

In the second part of the sequence the poet concentrates on the actual potatoes, describing their germination, their colour and shape. Taking them out of the soil is compared to a birth but heaped in the pit they are like skulls.

Adopting a sing-song rhythm the poet, in part three, tells of a blight that struck the potatoes causing famine throughout the country. When picked the roots were firm but in the air they rotted. Unable to find any food the people saw their hopes dwindling to grief. The countryside stank of decaying potatoes and the memory of the famine persists today.*

* See 'Historical background' in Part 1 for details of the famine.

The final part depicts the gatherers of the first part now taking their lunch. When they have finished eating they cast their leftovers on the ground like offerings to the earth goddess.

COMMENTARY: The personal recollections explored in 'Digging' are now broadened to a historical perspective. The traditional regularity of the potato digging is a ritual. Memories of the famine remind the people of the power the earth wields over their life and death. They revere it as a god:

> Centuries
> Of fear and homage to the famine god
> Toughen the muscles behind their humbled knees,

Human figures are diminished by the size of this god. In the opening verse they 'swarm' like insects, and in the next verse their movements are as awkward as the flight of crows. Describing the soil as 'surf' the poet draws a parallel between the power of earth and that of the sea.

The potatoes are given an animal life in the second part as they breed like rabbits in a 'hutch', and seem like hearts that have hardened in the earth. Again the poet relishes their physical aspect. This fecundity and the nourishment offered by the potatoes is reversed in the final double paradox: 'live skulls, blind-eyed'. The characteristic black spots on potatoes are commonly referred to as 'eyes' so the accuracy of the description 'blind-eyed' reinforces the image of the skulls.

This image dominates the next part of the poem and the 'higgledy line' of the diggers from the first part becomes a horde of 'higgledy skeletons'. The reversal implied in Part II is furthered by the shift from 'petrified hearts' to 'putrefied' potatoes, and the earth, first seen as a mother, is now a 'bitch'. It is to this unreliable deity that the workers continue to offer their homage in the last section. The corresponding image of the sea is recalled by the hovering 'flotilla of gulls'.

The action in each part of the poem is reflected in the varying rhythms. A consistent decasyllabic line and an *abab* rhyme scheme in the first conveys the sense of repetitive gesture implied in the phrase 'Processional stooping'. For Part II this regular structure is replaced by a free verse rendering the irregular shape of the potatoes. The grotesquery of the images inspired by the famine is increased by jaunty rhymed couplets:

> In a million wicker huts
> beaks of famine snipped at guts.

Their sing-song effect impresses them on the memory of the reader just as the famine is impressed on the memory of the poet and his people. The easier rhythm of the present returns in the final section with the regular structure of Part I.

Those forces that menaced the poet's environment in 'Digging' and

'Death of a Naturalist' are here given a real and historical basis. The potato diggers fear that just as the seasons return so too might the famine.

NOTES AND GLOSSARY:

wicker:	basketwork, woven of twigs
creel:	large basket
'forty-five:	1845, the first year of the famine
flotilla:	fleet of small ships
dead-beat:	(*colloquial*) exhausted

'The Diviner' *Death of a Naturalist*

The first words of this poem form its title and the first verse continues with a description of the diviner's preparations. Holding a branch from a hazel bush he walks around the field and waits for the stiffening movement of the rod that will indicate a hidden source of water.

When this strange signal comes, the poet compares it to the aerial transmission of radio waves.

Onlookers ask to hold the rod. In silence the diviner gives it to them but it remains limp in their hands. If he holds their wrists it moves again of its own accord.

COMMENTARY: Many of Heaney's poems refer back to a period when farm work was chiefly manual and the rural community depended on the talents of men such as the water-diviner. This talent has a mystical quality, with the man acting as a medium for the magnetic liaison between the hidden water and the hazel rod.

Consistent with this mysticism is the adverbial levity of the vocabulary. The silent patience of the diviner is emphasised by the placing of the final word of the first sentence. Stretched across the gap between two verses the description 'professionally/Unfussed' heightens the suspense of waiting and the sense of mystery. The delay also heightens the effect of the surprising central image in the second verse.

Rhymes fall regularly on the final words of each line in an *abab* sequence. By its position at the end of the second line and by its rhyme with 'professionally' the letter V is given the status of a word. Standing as an emblem of the rod it takes on some of its mysterious properties.

For Heaney the diviner's performance represented 'pure technique', and speaking of this poem he referred to Sir Philip Sidney's* definition

---

* Sir Philip Sidney (1554–86), the son of a Viceroy of Ireland, is generally regarded as the ideal Elizabethan gentleman. His influence is chiefly literary, his political career having been cut short by his death in battle. His *Defence of Poesie* initiated a renaissance of English literature and his *Arcadia* is the first original English work of prose fiction. With the sequence *Astrophel and Stella* he introduced the Petrarchan sonnet cycle to England.

of the poet as 'vates'. In this classical image the poet is a man possessed of profound insight, like a seer or priest. Heaney discerns a poetic resonance in the coincidence of 'word' and 'stirred' in the final verse. Thus, the power of the diviner is transferred to the poet and the attraction of the water is located in the word.

'Personal Helicon' *Death of a Naturalist*

This is the final poem in *Death of a Naturalist*. The Helicon of its title refers to the mountain on which, in Greek mythology, the nine muses lived. The water in the streams running down its sides had the power to inspire the gift of poetry in those who drank it.

Seamus Heaney locates this poetic source in farmyard wells. When he was a child nothing could be done to stop him leaning over their rims. He was attracted by the darkness and the rank smells. In each verse a different well is described. As he grows older the boy sees further into the wells and looks for his reflection. He hears his voice returning with a musical sound. A rat running across the surface of a well frightens him. Now the poet rejects these childish obsessions and says that he will come to know himself by writing poetry instead.

COMMENTARY: As in 'Digging' the opening descriptions of this poem build up towards a definition of the poet's approach to his writing. It is through his senses rather than his intellect that he discovers the desire to compose poetry. The sound of his voice echoing in the dark has a 'clean new music' and in the final verse the substance of 'slime' is linked to the quality of 'rhyme':

> Now, to pry into roots, to finger slime
> To stare, big-eyed Narcissus, into some spring
> Is beneath all adult dignity. I rhyme
> To see myself, to set the darkness echoing.

Danger lurks here too, for he still risks a fall into the darkness, this time of the self.

'The Forge' *Door into the Dark*

The dark interior of the forge provokes the poet's curiosity. Around its door lie discarded pieces of ironwork. He can only guess at the activity inside by the noises he hears. There is the bell-like sound of the anvil being hammered, followed by a glimpse of the showering sparks and the sizzle of the hot shoe being plunged into water.

He knows that the anvil stands in the middle of the workshop, its pointed end like the horn of a unicorn. It is fixed into place and the poet thinks of it as an altar where the blacksmith devotes himself to his art.

The blacksmith comes to the door of his forge where he watches for a moment as the cars go by. He remembers a time when the only traffic was that of horse-drawn carts. Impatient with this changed order he returns to his task of forging durable iron.

COMMENTARY: The title for Seamus Heaney's second collection of verse is taken from the opening line of this poem. The real subject of 'The Forge' is the sacred nature of art, associated here with the skilful work of the blacksmith.

The anvil, positioned in the middle of the forge, is located too at the centre of the poem, its permanence and stillness emphasised by the placing of the colon:

> The anvil must be somewhere in the centre,
> Horned as a unicorn, at one end square,
> Set there immoveable: an altar

The open sounds of 'somewhere'/'square'/'altar' prepare a space in which the assonance of 'horned as a unicorn' acquires a concrete sound.

In the sudden double image of the unicorn and the altar the three areas of meaning in the poem are co-ordinated. By comparing the anvil to the mythical beast the poet alludes to the world of medieval romance. Working at this altar the blacksmith is like a priest. The poet stands at the edge of a similar dedication, staring into the darkness of the unknown.

The decline in the demand for the blacksmith's work suggested at the opening by the sight of the rusting axles and hoops is confirmed in the last lines by the contrast between the 'flashing' traffic and the solidity of the iron. The blacksmith continues to work, nonetheless, maintaining a faith in the superiority of his material.

'The Forge' is composed in the form of a sonnet. Division into octet and sextet is marked by a shift of focus from the forge to the blacksmith. The poet does not adhere to the iambic pentameter throughout and there is an echo of Gerard Manley Hopkins in the sprung rhythm of 'the hammered anvil's short-pitched ring', setting up a tempo that suits the action of the blacksmith.

'Requiem for the Croppies'   *Door into the Dark*

Written for the fiftieth anniversary of the 1916 rising this poem recounts an incident from the rebellion of 1798.*

* See 'Historical background' in Part 1.

The poet speaks with the voice of a band of men, led by a priest, who fought the government troops in Wexford. Their tactics were improvised to suit the terrain as they moved through fields and ditches, never making camp. The only weapons they had were pikes. By driving cattle into a stampede they could create the effect of a battle charge. For sustenance they filled their pockets with barley.

Despite their ingenuity these farmhands turned soldiers were eventually beaten. Scythes were no match for the cannon of the enemy. The poet envisages their death as a wave of blood pouring down the hill (Vinegar Hill outside Enniscorthy) on which they made their last stand on 21 June 1798. Here they were buried and in August of the same year a crop of barley grew up from the seeds in their pockets.

COMMENTARY: The political content of this poem is summarised in the final image of a crop springing from a grave. This seasonal renewal anticipates another rising. As in 'At a Potato Digging' the poet here combines the recurrence of the seasons with a historical event. The agricultural basis of his society gives him a cyclical view of history.

The hasty progress of the croppies is emulated by the frequent use of punctuational dashes and irregular line lengths. The pace is speeded up too by the absence of an internal pattern (there is very little use of alliteration or assonance). Repeated statements such as 'No kitchens ... no striking camp—'/'We moved ... '/'We found ... '/'We'd cut ... ' provide a rhythm that impels the reader to the end of the line where a regular rhyme scheme sustains the momentum.

'Undine'   *Door into the Dark*

The speaker of this poem is the female spirit of water. She tells of how the farmer has cleared ditches and drains allowing her to run again. She speaks with the allure of a seductive woman drawing attention to her nakedness after the drains have been cleared.

A new irrigation channel is dug by the farmer into which the water runs, effecting a sexual union with him through his land. She seeps into the soil and nourishes his crop. In this process she is touched by his desire and becomes human.

COMMENTARY: The significance of this poem is twofold. First, the poet here assumes a female persona, a device which he will employ in subsequent poems. Through this voice he dramatises that part of himself where the creative urge arises. The farmer's relation to the water is equivalent to the poet's dependence on his muse.

The female voice overlays the verbs 'rippled and churned' with a cajoling innuendo. The union of the farmer and his land is played out in the *aa bb* rhyme scheme of the last four lines, contrasting with the preceding unrhymed lines.

The second significant aspect of this poem is its method of composition. Citing Eliot's* theory of the 'auditory imagination' Heaney explains how 'Undine' grew from the single word of its title:

> It was the dark pool of the sound of the word that first took me, if our auditory imaginations were sufficiently attuned to plumb and sound a vowel, to unite the most primitive and civilised associations, the word 'undine' would probably suffice as a poem in itself.†

His sensitivity to origins implicit in the sound of a word has developed out of the poet's preference for concrete and imitative words.

In this description Heaney has defined a tension fundamental in his work. Throughout his poems instinct, the preserve of primitive feeling, is counteracted by intellect, the touchstone of civilisation.

NOTES AND GLOSSARY:

Undine: a water spirit that becomes human on giving birth to a human child

---

'The Wife's Tale'	*Door into the Dark*

Here too the speaker is a woman. She brings food to the field for her husband and his helpers. Having laid it on a cloth on the ground she tells them it is ready. The threshing machine stops and the only sound to be heard is that of the men walking across the stubble.

Her husband lies on the grass and tells her to feed the other men first. He admires the cloth, remarking that only a woman would be so meticulous. Men, he says, have no need of such things. He watches her pouring his tea and serving the bread to his taste. He is satisfied with the seed and tells her to look at it. She never knows how to assess its quality.

She feels it and compares the texture to small bullets. The bags hang open at the end of the chutes. She walks back between the pitchforks that stand like javelins on a battlefield.

The men have finished their meal and lie in silence, smoking. With pride her husband confirms that the seed is good. She knows she is no longer wanted, and, taking the cups and cloth, she leaves. The men stay as they were, resting in the shade.

---

* T.S. Eliot (1888–1965) was an American poet who spent most of his working life in England and became a British citizen. His influence extends from poetry and poetic drama to literary history and criticism. His most innovative and best-known work is the long poem *The Waste Land*. His theory of the 'auditory imagination' is proposed in the study *The Use of Poetry and the Use of Criticism* (1933). He worked in the London publishing house of Faber and Faber.

† 'Feeling into Words', *Preoccupations*, p.52.

COMMENTARY: This woman's view of the world is like that of the boy in 'Death of a Naturalist'. She reads her environment through her senses: she is alert to the sound of the men's approach and she judges the seed by its feel in her hands. Like the boy she finds menace in the world. The threshing machine is monstrous with its 'hum and gulp' and its 'jaws' spewing straw. Weapon imagery reinforces this threatening atmosphere: the seed is like 'shot', the pitchforks like 'javelins' making the stubble field a 'battlefield'.

Most intimidating of all, however, is her husband's arrogance. Her actions are dictated by his needs; she serves his food and inspects the seed. He is presumptuous, 'as proud as if he were the land itself', and dismisses her when she has performed her duties. The title of the poem reflects his mocking attitude. To say of a belief or superstition that it is 'an old wives' tale' is to reject it as having no basis in fact. In her submissive silence (only the husband's words are reported) the wife conceals her foreboding and resentment. She fears to have her feelings mocked as the cloth was.

Unlike the 'Undine', this woman is repressed. The masculine images of arms and battle betray a rebellious instinct on her part.

'A Lough Neagh Sequence' _Door into the Dark_

Arranged in seven parts this sequence draws on the experience of the eel-fishers from Ardboe in County Tyrone.

1. 'Up the Shore'. The local lore surrounding the lake is related here. Fishermen believe that one of their number must be drowned each year. It is said that the water of the lake can make wood as hard as stone, and that it conceals a ruined town. The Isle of Man is said once to have filled the space where the lake is now.

At the lower end of the lake a dam has been built to trap the incoming eels, providing a haul of up to five hundred. Further inland the fishermen work by the old method. By never learning to swim they put themselves at a disadvantage equal to that of the eels. They dismiss the risk they take by saying that they will die more quickly. Although storms rarely strike and they are never far from the shore they insist that the lake must have its annual victim.

2. 'Beyond Sargasso'. The male eel journeys through the Atlantic to his breeding ground. Having crossed the ocean he comes inland through river estuaries. His instinct is like the gravity that keeps a planet in its orbit. Nothing inhibits his advance. He moves like an icicle enlarging itself with new melting layers. Finally he burrows into the shore as a root in the earth. He has come here hungry for a mate and will be stopped only by spades and oars.

3. 'Bait'. Working in silence, the men feel under leaves and grass for the worms that will bait their lines. The worms will be caught when they begin to relax back into their tunnels. The poet imagines the worms making piles of mud like crowns as they aerate the soil. Some will certainly be caught by the fishermen hunting at night.

4. from 'Setting'. With worms fixed to their hooks the men pay the line out over the side of the boat. Under the water it is invisible and forgotten. The line straightens and the boat moves forward, the oars turning as the eels circle around the bait.

5. 'Lifting'. The boat drifts northwards with its engine switched off. The men draw in the line heavy and darkened with eels. Not all of the hooks have been taken. An eel is as wide as a man's wrist.

Hooks are left in their mouths as the eels are taken from the line and thrown into a barrel. There they wind themselves together like balls of wool. They take on a single oily shape absorbing each fresh catch. In the same way trails of foam behind the boats criss-cross so that it is impossible to see the single trail of one boat.

If the fishermen are asked when the custom of fishing for eels began they will reply that it started with the season.

6. 'The Return'. The female eel leaves the breeding ground. Driven by hunger she swims through every waterway she encounters. The poet wonders if she is aware of her route. She passes along the north coast leaving no trail. Once at sea, in the place where she was born, she releases her own eggs.

7. 'Vision'. In his childhood people warned the poet that he should comb his hair, to prevent the head-lice forming a rope and dragging him into the water.

This made him wary of water. He thought that he could see the rope in the grass bent by the wind. When he was older he watched the eels moving at night in the grass and thought that his fears had come to life. That insight reinforces the old superstition.

COMMENTARY: Just as the potato diggers described above (see p.24) treated the earth with reverence so too the eel-fishers regard the lake as a god demanding the annual tribute of a human life.

Cycles are repeated throughout the sequence, the seasonal progression of time, the return of the eels to their breeding- and hatching-grounds and of the poet's memory to his childhood. All move in a cosmic unison suggested by the comparison of the eel to a planet in Part 2 and the image of the worms clothed by the earth in Part 3. The circle is closed by the 'girdle' of time in 'Vision'. Underlying this metaphorical structure is the constant circular movement of the eels in Parts 2, 4 and 6.

The individual poems are linked by the thread-like shapes of the eels, worms, fishing lines and the wake of the boats. The poet is consciously invoking the circle as the archetypal emblem of fertility.

The form of each part of the sequence alters according to its subject. Part 1, consisting of four numbered verses, provides a chronicle of the lake's history. Unqualified assertions echo the enigmatic talk of the fishermen in the opening assertion which is confirmed by its repetition in quotation marks at the end of Part 1: 'The lough will claim a victim every year.' This formal shape is supported by a regular rhyme scheme.

By contrast Parts 2 and 6 emulate the shape of the eels within long narrow verses and a syllabic metre. In Part 3, 'Bait', rhythms of speech are set against poetic diction. Phrases such as 'follow their nose', 'Nab him but wait', 'draw steady and he'll come' have a colloquial sound. An archaic vocabulary and syntax are deployed through a single long sentence in the second half of the poem. A repeated line in the first and last verses and a repeated half line in the fourth and fifth create a choric effect. The *abb* rhyme is broken only in the third verse where the *aba* sequence imitates the pinching action of the man's fingers on the worm. With these devices the poet obliquely juxtaposes the traditions of poetry and fishing. Parts 3, 4 and 5 are linked by the use of the same form and metre.

In its original version 'Setting' included a second part in which the ritual aspect of fishing was stressed by a comparison with the order of the Catholic mass. Omitting this reference here Seamus Heaney emphasises the mystery inherent in the skill of fishing. This mystery is implied in the colloquial phrase 'out of sight out of mind' associating the lake with the subconscious.

Childhood fears are revived for the poet in 'Vision':

Every time the wind passed. Years
Later in the same fields
He stood at night when eels
Moved through the grass like hatched fears

The rhyme of 'years' and 'fears' at the end of the lengthened lines implies an annual renewal of fear such as the danger anticipated by the fishermen in Part 1. The instinctive revulsion of the child as expressed in the metaphysical structure of the last verse, is equally potent for the adult.

In the shape of the eels the poet confronts the image of his own sexuality. As in 'Death of a Naturalist' the reproductive cycle is loaded with danger. The fertility referred to in this sequence is both physical and imaginative. Allusions to the subconscious and the use of a poetic vocabulary culminate in 'Vision'. Fear acts as a goad to the poet's imagination and curiosity drives him to probe the menace of the dark.

'Bogland'	*Door into the Dark*

The poet here compares the tracts of bog in Ireland to the prairies of America. The bog brings the horizon close, unlike the wide view of the prairies.

One is forced to look downwards at a bog, to peer into the small pools that gather in its holes. Under the sun the turf dries till it is like bread. Acid in the soil of the bog has a preservative action and ancient remains have been found there including the skeleton of the now extinct great Irish Elk. People used to bury butter in the bog to keep it fresh. This too has been found over a century later. The poet likens the bog to butter. It is so soft that it is impossible to determine its age by the usual method of counting layers of soil.

This ground is too soft to yield coal. The bog is, however, a source of fuel formed by the compacted decay of old vegetation. The depth of the bog corresponds to the width of the prairie. The men who dig for turf are like the pioneers who settled on the American plains. It is so deep that its water may have been absorbed from the Atlantic ocean. Local superstition holds that the centre of the bog is bottomless.

COMMENTARY: The poet's resolution to 'dig' with his pen is realised in this poem as he delves into the darkness that underpins his second collection of verse.

Personal memory widens here into racial memory, a shift that is marked by the communal persona of 'we' and 'our'. The poem moves through a sequence of short sentences spoken in an informal tone with regular use of the possessive pronoun: 'We have . . . ', 'Our unfenced country . . . ', 'Our pioneers . . . '. The diggers and archaeologists are likewise referred to in a familiar way as 'They'. Classical allusion is grounded in the colloquial as the poet compares the 'tarns' or pools in the bog to the 'cyclops' eye'.

A mnemonic effect is created by the repetition of certain images and sounds; for example, the human 'eye' is reflected by the 'cyclops' eye' and in the 'sights' of the bog. Time is told in centuries and millennia. Negative statements and paradox provide a linguistic correlative for the hidden area of the bog:

Melting and opening underfoot
Missing its last definition
By millions of years.
They'll never dig coal here

Instead, out of these depths comes the Elk, paradoxically like a 'crate full of air'.

Seamus Heaney has said that this was the first of his poems to have the resonance of a symbol. An awareness of the bog is ingrained into the mind of all Irish children for they are taught that Ireland is shaped like a saucer, with a mountainous coast and a bog at the centre. Thus, the use of the first person plural by the poet reflects this communal consciousness. The bog corresponds to the deepest area of memory and imagination where cycles of history coincide and are retained.

This poem closes with a reference to two local superstitions. Consider their effect here and compare it with the use of superstition in other poems from *Door into the Dark*.

COMMENTARY: This poem is dedicated to T.P. Flanagan (*b*. 1929), a northern Irish painter and teacher of art. He is a friend of Seamus Heaney. In the 1960s he worked on a series of 'Bogland' studies. The poet watched him make some of the preparatory drawings for the series.

'Broagh' *Wintering Out*

This poem is a description of the images and memories conjured by the place name of its title.

A field beside the river is bordered by dock leaves and a sheltered path that leads to the crossing in the river. The ground is soft and water collected in a footprint makes a round pond like the O in Broagh. The sound of that O is like a breeze in the elderberry trees and the leaves of the rhubarb.

Ending in a guttural Irish sound the word is not an easy one for foreigners to pronounce.

COMMENTARY: The poems of *Wintering Out* are filled with ghostly shapes. Among these the chief ghost is the Irish language. No longer spoken by the poet's people it only remains in dialect words and place names. One such is 'Broagh', a townland straddled by the farm on which the poet grew up.

There is an old Irish tradition of writing 'Dinnseanchas' or place-name poems describing topographical details. Here, in his description of the place, Seamus Heaney succeeds in emulating the sound of its name by the long 'o's of the third verse:

> its low tattoo
> among the windy boortrees
> and rhubarb-blades

This sound has the effect almost of eliding the final 'gh' of 'Broagh'.

The vocabulary of this poem reflects the mixed linguistic and, thereby, the mixed racial heritage of the poet. 'Docken' is an old English plural form and 'rigs' is a Scottish word introduced by the settlers in the seventeenth century.

This and other place-name poems such as 'Anahorish' pleased the poet because through them he succeeded in transposing the resonance of the Irish language into English, his own first language.

NOTES AND GLOSSARY:
boortrees: elderberry trees

'Traditions'   *Wintering Out*

Depicting the Irish tongue as a female 'muse' the poet describes its forced mating with the English literary style. Those Irish words that have survived are useless, like parts of the human anatomy that bear witness to evolution, or like a rushwork cross left hanging in a shed. The social order too has changed and the poet's community is subject to an English monarch.

A seventeenth-century English vocabulary persists in the English spoken in Ireland, with words such as 'varsity', 'deem' and 'allow'. Other unusual words give this Hiberno-English a Shakespearean quality. The dialects of some regions are distinguished by a consonantal sound, and people are divided by their use of the words 'bawn' and 'mossland', introduced by Scottish and English planters.

In Part 3 the poet brings together two fictional Irishmen. MacMorris, a character in William Shakespeare's (1564–1616) *Henry V,* answers the jibes of his comrades by trying to define his own nation. The definition is eventually supplied by Leopold Bloom, one of the principal characters of James Joyce's *Ulysses* (1922). Bloom's doubts are resolved when he says that his nation is the place where he was born, Ireland.

COMMENTARY: The cultural dualism of Heaney's background can be the cause of acute confusion to the poet. To which literary tradition does he truly belong: the original Gaelic or the later Anglo-Saxon one? The two are summarised by their sounds, the 'guttural' Gaelic and the 'alliterative' English. Like the uvula and the coccyx the Irish language is present but ignored, and devotion to one of the patron saints of Ireland is replaced by adherence to English customs.

The English that the poet speaks has, nonetheless, a distinctive character. Technically known as Hiberno-English, it is distinguished by the simultaneous preservation of seventeenth-century forms (the period when English influence in Ireland was strongest) and of loan-words such as 'bawn' and 'moss' introduced by Scottish and English settlers. 'Mossbawn' was the name of the poet's home. Heaney has commented that in his pronunciation of the English word 'bawn' there is the sound of the Irish word 'ban' meaning white. He takes this to refer to the white bog cotton plant, and he adds:

In the syllables of my home I see a metaphor of the split culture of Ulster.*

It was James Joyce who first exploited the diversity of Hiberno-English and, by concluding with the words of Leopold Bloom, Heaney also acknowledges the literary possibilities inherent in his language. The phrase 'anatomies of death' alludes to another literary source, Edmund Spenser's *View of the Present State of Ireland*.†

The technical linguistic content of this and other poems in *Wintering Out* has prompted the use of a more scientific vocabulary by the poet. Linguistics, evolution and anatomy provide him with words such as 'guttural' and 'alliterative', 'vestigial', 'coccyx' and 'uvula'. Their effect is counteracted by vernacular phrases like 'grass-roots stuff'.

The voice the poet projects here is the communal one introduced in 'Bogland', and the connection between landscape and memory made in that poem is continued here by the correspondence between accent and environment.

'The Tollund Man'   *Wintering Out*

The poet undertakes to go to Aarhus, a town in Denmark, where he will see the preserved body of an Iron Age man. He describes the body from a photograph. Seeds from the man's last meal remain in his stomach. The only garment he wears is a cap, and ropes are tied around his waist and neck. Already mesmerised, the poet longs to see the actual body.

It is thought that the man was sacrificed in a ritual marriage to the goddess of fertility. The bog, her body, engulfed and protected his body. He is like a saint miraculously preserved.

Although it is blasphemous, the poet looks on the bog as a holy place and prays to the Tollund man. He wants some good to come out of the sectarian killings in his homeland, where ugly bodies with torn flesh lie in farmyards. He pictures too the bodies of four brothers murdered on a railway line. By contrast the Tollund man is tranquil.

On his journey the poet imagines that he will feel the same mixture of regret and honour that filled the Iron Age man on the way to his death. He names the places through which he will pass. People will point at him as they once did at the Tollund man but the poet will be separated from them by his ignorance of their language.

* 'Belfast', *Preoccupations*, p.35.
† Edmund Spenser (?1552−99), the author of the long patriotic allegorical poem *The Faerie Queene*. He lived for a time in Ireland and was commissioned by Queen Elizabeth I to report on the situation there during the Munster rebellion. This report, quoted by Seamus Heaney, was entitled *View of the Present State of Ireland*. It is quoted in Heaney's 'Bog Oak' as well.

His mood there will be one of mixed sadness and familiarity. In a foreign country he will discern traces of the same blood-letting practices that violate his society.

COMMENTARY: After writing 'Bogland' Seamus Heaney chanced upon a work entitled *The Bog People: Iron Age Man Preserved* by P.V. Glob. In this study of preserved bodies found in Danish and Irish bogs P.V. Glob concludes that they were victims sacrificed to the goddess of fertility. The male bodies were, it is thought, those of her priests wedded to her by the absolute submission of their life to hers.

Heaney's imagination was first stimulated by the photographs of these bodies. They provided an extension of his 'bogland symbol and the writing/digging metaphor'. 'The Tollund Man' and 'Nerthus' form a prelude to the 'Bog Poems' included in *North*.

In the opening section of 'The Tollund Man', the man's head is given a vegetable texture by its resemblance to 'peat' and seed 'pods', imagery that is echoed by the presence of undigested winter seeds in his stomach. The smallness of his head is defined by the short 'i's and alliterated 'p's of the monosyllabic words in the first verse. The balance of the initial and final 'p's in the fourth line seals the verse around the repose of the dead man.

Heaney describes writing this poem as having been a disturbing experience, for it provoked in him a 'sense of fear'. This fear arose out of his identification with the Tollund man, a process which begins in the third verse:

> Naked except for
> The cap, noose and girdle,
> I will stand a long time.
> Bridegroom to the goddess.

The punctuational break at the eleventh line of the poem (the third line in the verse above) is elided by the rhythm of the verse so that it reads as a comma and the 'I' becomes synonymous with the subsequent 'Bridegroom'. The rituals of neolithic society find an echo in the murders enacted in the poet's own society. In the third section he imagines himself as the victim about to be sacrificed.

The poet invokes the Tollund man as an emblem of a ritual order that is absent from the actions of those who kill in his society. The reverence that accompanied the death of the Tollund man is reflected in his restful posture and contrasts with contemporary victims. Reciting the names of the Danish towns through which he will travel the poet introduces the meditative rhythm of a prayer. His poetry is the pilgrimage that seeks an order to accommodate the persistent violent instincts of his people.

'Summer Home'	*Wintering Out*

The poet seeks to discover the cause of bad feeling between him and his wife.

He thinks that the smell of some rotting organism has soured their humour. The air seems to be infected. He follows the smell to its source under the mat. Relieved to have found it he cleans the area with boiling water. As he carries an armful of cut flowers indoors the poet hears the sound of his wife sobbing and saying his name. He recognises that the fault was his. Still holding the flowers the poet approaches his wife and sees in the blooms and their scent a token of a pious devotion to her. He entreats his wife to allow him to soothe the hurt he has caused.

Despite these intentions their love-making becomes a battle and leaves them stunned and separate. Again the poet finds himself trying to phrase or envisage a reconciliation. The clumsiness of these attempts contrasts with the natural grace of his wife's body in the shower. The harsh sound of an electric saw dividing logs and exposing their grained interior becomes a metaphor for the couple's return to their innermost feelings and the resulting strain on their emotions.

The humid air of a foreign summer makes the children restless. The poet and his wife argue and he accuses her of causing the rupture. All night they remain unyielding until the light of morning breaks into their room showing the ripeness of the corn and the creepers outside.

The poet recalls a moment of harmony from the previous day. In a cave they had tapped a stalactite and listened for the echo of its note. That sound provides an emblem of their love which, he says, rings as fine and true as the tone of a tuning fork.

COMMENTARY: With each section of this poem the poet recognises that the rancour between him and his wife runs deep. He looks at first for an external cause but when this fails he is driven in on himself. Finally he traces the source of their dispute to himself. The 'fouled nest' he sought in the first section is revealed now in his 'foul mouth'.

By the tone of each section the variations of his mood are registered and the free verse forms contribute to the impression of anxious uncertainty. His initial doubts and the need to allay them are expressed in the questions and in the insistent 'scald, scald, scald' of the first section. Following this aggressive action he is chastened by the private tears of his wife and her repetition of his name counterbalances the repeated 'scald'.

He adopts a poetic mannerism of self-accusation in the single line 'O love, here is the blame', emphasised by the rhyme of 'blame' and 'name'. He elaborates on his culpability in the prayerful vocabulary of the next verse: 'may altar', 'sweet chrism', 'Anoint'. The sanctity is, however, flawed by the word 'taint' which picks up the unsavoury atmosphere of Part I. His mannered tone returns in the concluding line with the imperatives 'Attend. Anoint the wound'.

This language of ritual is echoed in the final section where the word 'attend' is given an active significance as the dawn light moves in to restore the affection between the poet and his wife. It offers too the 'maize and vine', emblems of fertility, in place of the scented flowers of Part II.

Despite his annoyance the poet regards his wife with reverence. In Part II the flowers are like those traditionally offered to the Blessed Virgin in the month of May. His wife's easy movements in Part III contrast with his self-conscious gestures towards 'thick healings'. The word 'stoups', applied to her breasts, refers to vessels for holy water and is overlaid by its resemblance to the word 'stoops' which parallels the bending of her body in the shower.

Reverence turns to aggression in the colloquial thrust of the pun 'we tented' on 'Attend'. The word 'homely' too is imbued with irony when the images of the wound and the tent provide the context for a battle, until the poet and his wife lie shocked by their mutual violence. This aggression finds another form in the action of the saw in Part IV.

The inward return described in Part IV is dramatised at the end of Part V where the poet discovers harmony in the cave. The primitive simplicity of this image provided an unexpected antidote to the couple's bitterness and contrasts with the aggressive and aesthetic resolutions that conclude each previous section.

'Westering'   *Wintering Out*

In this poem written in California, the poet looks back on his journey from Ireland to America. He looks at the Official Map of the Moon by Rand McNally and remarks on its likeness to the skin of a frog with craters like opened pores. 'Pitiscus' is the name of one which catches his eye. This scientific map, however, sets him to remembering the time before his departure from Ireland.

Moonlight projected his shadow onto a whitewashed wall in a farmyard. Now he compares this light to the shine of bones which makes the cobblestones look like eggs. All summer he had progressed towards California like a parachutist who waits until the last minute to open his parachute. Finally he landed in the barren landscape of the west of Ireland, the taking-off point for America.

He and his family departed on Good Friday. Shops were closed that day as a mark of reverence and all the people were gathered inside the churches. The poet's passage through these places was only a brief distraction like the sound of bells on the altar. At the sound of the bells the worshippers bow before the crucifix. The poet is aware of blasphemy in his action for it is not considered right to travel on a Good Friday. As the journey continues the roads seem to drop away behind him like fishing lines being lowered into the water.

The figure of Christ is replaced by that of the moon which manifests the same spontaneously bleeding wounds as Christ. The poet fuses this moonscape with the memory of his home and compares the disruption his blasphemy has caused (in the seventh verse) with the effect of the moon's zero gravity, displacing the body of Christ on the cross.

COMMENTARY: Viewing the map of the moon does not inspire wonder at a new world in the poet but instead gives him a new perspective on himself and on the moonlit farmyards which provide the setting for so many of the poems in *Wintering Out*. He looks back now as the moon does on the earth, seeing his own shadow and the reflection of the light on the cobbles.

The closing poem in each of Heaney's first four collections involves an advance towards something new. In 'Westering' he equates the journey from Ireland to California with a journey to the moon. The journey is presented in a series of present participles reproducing the buoyant effect of losing gravity: 'dwindling', 'Falling', 'loosening'. These are supplemented by others such as: 'Recalling', 'Ending', 'shining', 'weighing'. His own loss of gravity is reflected in the effect of his blasphemy which causes the body of Christ to slip from the cross.

Heaney has referred to this poem as an example of the free verse techniques he learnt when in California. This new form is evident in the dilating line lengths, the use of dashes and the infrequent end-rhyme. These features accentuate the apparently random associations made through the poem:

Its enlarged pores held

Open and one called
'Pitiscus' at eye level—
Recalling the last night
In Donegal, my shadow

Within this free style, however, patterns of sound are played out; for example in the verse above there is the echoing fall of 'called', 'Recalling', 'Donegal' and the rhyme of 'held' and 'called'. The lunar place-name 'Pitiscus' is balanced by the local name 'Donegal'. A relaxed conversational rhythm is set up by the movement from 'I' in the first verse to 'We' at the centre of the poem and back to 'I' at the end.

The changes wrought by his journey are monitored by the shifting mood and meaning of certain words: 'Lit' in the third verse gives way to the other meaning of 'light' as referring to weight in the eighth verse; 'shine' becomes 'shining' and 'free fall' becomes 'Falling', the precise effect of the former giving way to the vague sound of the latter. Phrases are set down like notes for the description of a larger scene, for example the closed shops and the parked cars and bicycles present a scene devoid of people. Long sentences broken into alternating long and short lines suggest a leisurely pace imitative of the long slow journey the poem describes.

'Mossbawn: Two Poems in Dedication'   *North*

These poems are dedicated to the poet's aunt and to the memory of his family home at Mossbawn.

1. 'Sunlight'. The farmyard is still and empty in the sunlight which warms the iron water pump. Catching the reflection of the sun, water in a bucket looks as thick as honey. A patch of light on the wall resembles a baking tray left out to cool. In the kitchen a woman is baking. As the cooker heats it reddens, sending a wave of warmth against her body. She works beside the window and wears an apron dusty with flour.

When she has finished preparing the dough she dusts the board with a feather brush and sits down. Her finger nails are white from work and her shins are mottled by the heat. There is a peaceful atmosphere in the kitchen as she waits for the scones to bake, and the only sound is the ticking of two clocks. Love is tangible in this stillness and the poet compares its constancy to the worn hand-shovel buried in the meal bin.

COMMENTARY: Introducing this poem at a reading Seamus Heaney described it as an attempt to write from the point of view of a foetus in the womb. Sensations of heat and light predominate and the mood evoked is one of tranquillity.

By applying only images that fit the scene, water as honey, sunlight as a griddle, the poet encloses the speaker within an atmosphere of domestic calm. This succession of images contributes to the surprising effect of the final verse:

> And here is love
> like a tinsmith's scoop
> sunk past its gleam
> in the meal bin.

The lasting quality of maternal love epitomised by the durable tin shovel fills the timeless interval that falls between the two clocks in the preceding verse. The tin is hidden from the transfiguring light of the sun.

The free verse style used by the poet at the end of *Wintering Out* is applied here as the line lengths fluctuate and end-rhymes are incidental. The 'absence' referred to in the first line is gradually infiltrated by the presence of objects in the yard and finally of the woman in the kitchen. By its long narrow shape the poem emulates the 'long after-noon'. Through its lines the long 'o' sounds of 'stood', 'cooling', 'afternoon', 'goose's' build towards the 'tinsmith's scoop' and the short 'o's of 'iron', 'honeyed', 'long', 'stove', 'apron', 'scone' lead into 'love'. An expectant mood is conveyed by the images of waiting; the pump, the water, the sunlight and the woman are strung together on the line of narrow verses, all composed in the process of baking.

2. 'The Seed Cutters'. In the opening line the poet invokes the spirit of the Flemish painter Jan Breughel (*c.* 1520–69) and by doing so casts his poem in a pictorial style. The labourers seems to belong to another era. They crouch under a hedge, sheltering from the wind. Their task is to cut the seed potatoes.

Small potatoes are distinguished by the dainty shape of their leaves, and the roots are protected under a bed of straw. The work proceeds slowly. The men split the potatoes and watch them fall open to reveal a stain of water at their centre.

The poet addresses the seasonal round as a god and asks that the tasks which it governs may endure. He would like the members of his community to be recorded as perpetuators of an ancient tradition.

COMMENTARY: As in 'Sunlight' the mood here is of timelessness and continuity. Two time-scales, the chronological one of 'hundreds of years' and the cyclical one of 'calendar customs', correspond to the tick-ing of the clocks in the previous poem. By invoking Breughel, a sixteenth-century painter of proverbs and seasons, the poet accentuates this effect.

The scene depicted is reminiscent of that in the final section of 'At a Potato Digging' and in 'The Wife's Tale'. The poet has, in this sequence, drawn from the same source, extended it from a specifically Irish con-text to a continental European one, and ultimately he identifies himself with the people who are his subject.

A deliberate pattern of repetitions fixes the scene and expresses the indolence of the men. Sentences begin with 'they': 'They seem', 'They kneel', 'They are'. The fourth line has a reflexive structure with 'wind-break' varied by 'wind is breaking'. The sentence running from the seventh into the eighth line combines two related colloquial expres-sions: 'time to kill' and 'taking their time'. The poet's use of the sonnet form parallels the farmers' adherence to long-established practices.

These two poems are a placatory prelude to the violent themes of the succeeding poems.

'Funeral Rites'   *North*

In this three-part poem the poet searches for a ritual that will contain the anger and grief that follow upon a death by violence.

His role as a coffin-bearer at the funerals of his relatives is recalled as a part of his initiation into manhood. Tradition demanded that the body be washed and displayed where relatives and friends could come to pay their last respects to the dead person.

The rooms would be darkened and odorous, the faces of the dead shone and the hands looked white and plump as dough. Rosary beads were twined around the fingers. The poet remembers especially the stretched skin on the swollen hands. Fingernails had discoloured and the wrists were posed as if for prayer.

He would kneel in front of the body which was dressed in a brown robe and laid upon a satin quilt. The room was candlelit, the wax dribbled and the flames flickered as women moved about. In one corner stood the lid of the coffin, its nails marked with crosses.

The poet's memory of these bodies is affectionate. Before the coffin lid was closed he would kiss the forehead. Then the funeral procession would move off.

He says that his community today lacks a ritual adequate to the shock and grief caused by sectarian murder. They need a practice ratified by tradition like the funerals described above. To this end he suggests reopening an ancient burial site in the centre of Ireland where all of these dead could be laid with dignity. He imagines the noise of thousands of cars reverberating about the countryside.

Women would remain at home, moving as if sleepwalking, following this procession in their minds. It would pass, the poet says, as quietly as a snake in the grass, its head reaching the tomb as its tail emerged from the north.

His choice of a pagan burial site prompts a reference to his country's ancient past. Certain place-names such as Strangford and Carlingford bear witness to their Norse foundation. The poet compares the ritual he has described with the practices of Old Norse society.

Satisfaction will be derived from the knowledge that these modern victims have been given an appropriate burial. The image of an ancient burial comes to the poet in the form of Gunnar, the hero of a Norse saga. Although Gunnar's death was not avenged as it should have been according to Norse law his body was seen sitting upright and unblemished inside his tomb. Here lit by candles the dead man sang of honour and looked at the moon.

COMMENTARY: A natural death is completed by the rituals of a wake and a funeral. The community is brought closer to the dead person and the usual routines of life are suspended to accommodate grief. In Heaney's description of the ceremony surrounding death the bodies appear to be restrained from proceeding towards another life, their hands are 'shackled' by the rosary beads and their wrists are 'obediently sloped'.

There is an element of worship in this 'waking' of the dead for the bodies have become statuesque, with 'eyelids glistening' and their faces like 'soapstone masks' with icy foreheads. In respect the mourners light candles, kneel and pray around the bodies and finally kiss their brows.

The want of a similar process for unnatural death is emphasised by the poet's paradoxical expression, 'neighbourly murder'. The usual convivial significance of 'neighbourly' is undermined by its association with 'murder'. The reliable structures of society are destroyed. In that paradox the despair of the community is summarised.

'Blinded' too in the next verse has a significant ambivalence; referring literally to the window blinds drawn shut as a mark of respect for the dead it carries the force of a physical affliction, implying that every family is in some way hurt by these murders.

The ritual that the poet would like to revive is a specifically pagan one, focused on a megalithic site in the centre of Ireland. The mound at Newgrange is thought by some to have been a passage grave. He reiterates his initial connection of funerals with virility when he envisages only men taking part in this new procession.

The image of the serpent has a particular meaning for the Irish reader. It is believed that St Patrick who introduced Christianity to Ireland banished snakes from the island. This was a symbolical purging of the demons of paganism. Now the poet reinvokes that primeval spirit in the attempt to formulate an alternative ritual.

To found such a ceremony would, he believes, lay memory to rest with the bodies of the dead. The site which he has chosen for this figurative burial has many historical associations. Of these the poet alludes to its proximity to the river Boyne, the scene of the crucial battle of 1690. The memory of this battle still rankles and provokes dissension in the poet's community. The capacity to remember is like a cud, chewing over old disputes.

The final image of comfort offered by the poet is drawn from the Old Norse text, *Njals Saga*. Occasional references, for example, 'black glacier', 'Strang and Carling fjords', the 'Gap of the North', have simultaneously guided the poem backwards and northwards into the poet's history. Gunnar's beauty in death parallels that of the poet's relatives.

Njals Saga is particularly appropriate in the context of this poem as it records the conflict between the old pagan way of life pursued by Gunnar and the new Christian ethos adopted by Njal. By the preservation of his memory in literature and his song of 'verses about honour' Gunnar sets a twofold example for Heaney. In his own verses the poet can ensure that the dead are remembered and he can resolve despair in an image of coherence.

Consider the relationship between memory and ritual in this poem and compare it with that in Heaney's other poems.

NOTES AND GLOSSARY:

dulse: a type of edible seaweed

cribs: beds

great chambers of Boyne: a group of megalithic mounds (the oldest dates from 3200BC), commonly believed to house burial chambers, or passage graves, though recent research suggests that they might have been temples of the sun. They are in the valley formed by the river Boyne in County Meath

cupmarked stones: stones associated with this site bearing a small rounded hollow

---

'Punishment'	*North*

The poet's contemplation here of another bog body leads him to reflect on the violent reprisals enacted in his own society.

At the outset he identifies himself with the dead girl, imagining the feel of the rope around her neck and the wind blowing against her skin. The wind stiffens her nipples making them hard as beads, and it makes her ribs tremble like the ropes and stays on a ship. He envisages her body submerged in the bog, weighed down by a stone and covered with branches.

When she was taken out of this hole she resembled a young tree stripped of its bark, her bones like branches, her brain like a fir cone. The poet compares her shorn head to a harvested field, and describes her blindfold as a protective binding. The rope about her neck he likens to a wedding ring.

He addresses her now as an adulteress, visualising her as she was before she died, blonde-haired and thin. Her face, now blackened by the bog, would have been beautiful. He pities her, recognising that she was a 'scapegoat', an object of blame for the community, punished for their sins.

His pity is close to love yet he realises that he too would have let her die, afraid to make his own sins known. Having acknowledged this the poet admits further to deriving a sexual thrill from his observation of the girl's naked body with its inner parts revealed. He has said nothing when girls in his society were punished for befriending English soldiers. Their heads too were shaved and covered in tar. Then the girls were tied to railings, their shame made public. Like those around him he has affected to deplore the act, aware that within himself he sympathises with the motive of revenge.

COMMENTARY: Like Gunnar the bog bodies are beautiful despite the violence of their deaths. Their long immersion in the bog has made them like natural objects. The parts of this girl's body are identified with native plants, her nipples are 'amber beads', she is a 'barked sapling', 'oak-bone', 'brain-firkin' and her shaved head is a field of stubble. The form in which these similes are presented is that of the 'kenning'. An Old English poetic device, the 'kenning' compresses the two elements of a simile to form a single image. The narrow shape of the poem is defined by the employment of these kennings in a style that underlines the Nordic associations of their subject.

Observation of the girl's exposed body turns the poet inward to himself to probe his own guilt.

> I almost love you
> but would have cast, I know,
> the stones of silence.

These 'stones of silence' refer to the incident in the New Testament of the woman taken in adultery (John 8: 1–12). As with the Pharisees the poet's silence is an acknowledgement of his own sins.

His self-accusation continues when he describes himself as a 'voyeur', deriving a perverse sexual thrill from the sight of the girl's body. More damning still is his silence when girls in his society have been punished for consorting with English soldiers. He has done nothing to prevent this happening but has joined his voice to the public expressions of horror. Thus he has concealed his instinctive sympathy for the ancient urge for retribution:

> who would connive
> in civilised outrage
> yet understand the exact
> and tribal, intimate revenge.

The internal rhyme of 'connive' and 'civilised' reinforces the poet's assertion that the public attitude is an agreed pose masking true feeling. The further sounding of the long 'i' in 'tribal' emphasises the contrast between the felt response and the spoken one. This dichotomy echoes that between the pagan and Christian procedures described in 'Funeral Rites'.

NOTES AND GLOSSARY:

amber:	petrified sap of trees found in Scandinavia
sapling:	a young tree
firkin:	a fir cone
flaxen:	the yellow colour of the flax plant
cauled:	caul, a covering for the head, also a membrane covering the scalp of a new-born child

'Kinship'	*North*

In six passages, each containing six four-lined verses, the poet anthologises the literal and metaphorical significance of the bog.

Through his familiarity with the bog he considers himself to be related to the corpses retrieved from its depths. The arrangements of drying turf are like a sacred script shared by him and these corpses.

Just as a domestic dog instinctively makes a nest before sleeping so the poet is naturally drawn to recover his past. When he walks on the bog the ground is unsteady and the water moving beneath his feet makes an elementary sound like a child's voice. He is attracted by the texture of the bog and he discerns in the pattern scored by troughs and ditches traces of the mysterious life that lies under its surface.

He enjoys, too, the sensation of walking on its soft ground and the sudden dip under the banks which is as surprising as the jerk of a body being hanged. The bog pools are like open jars, reflecting the moon as if they had swallowed it. They are so deep that their bottom cannot be seen.

In Part II the poet recites a litany of synonyms for the bog. He gives first a catalogue of the various English names for marshland and continues by describing it as the habitat of cold-blooded animals.

The word 'bog' itself is the Irish for 'soft' and is often used to denote a light rain. Inside the bog he discerns the presence of amber resembling the pupil of an eye. He endows the bog with animal qualities, seeing it as a stomach consuming snails and the shells of seeds. Here also pollen from the flowers is stored like grain.

It is like a kitchen cupboard and a tomb full of bones, it catches the sun and preserves offerings and the bodies of runaways with their swords still strapped to their sides. The bog resembles, too, a woman hungry for sex and will swallow swords like a circus performer. Jewels and rubbish are kept here. Replete with this accumulation of objects the bog is like an icy river carrying the evidence of human history in its stream.

This propensity for hoarding is likened by the poet to the action of his subconscious. Things remembered stay hidden there like bird's eggs in nests built under low hedges.

The poet finds a turf spade overgrown with a layer of moss. When he lifts the spade the moss opens like a mouth, making a low sound. The place where the spade lay is marked by a narrow brown ditch, like the moulted skin of an animal. The handle of the spade is damp and he stands it up in the air to dry.

Subsequently the poet discovers that a companion piece for the spade has been erected. An oak log split down its centre has been lifted from under a pile of stones and grass. The poet recognises the shape of the ancient goddess of the bogs.

The centre of the bog remains constant and spreads out into a large pool. Planted with seeds it is like an impregnated womb. In another aspect it is like a grave. Autumn makes the gound rank with the smell of rotting vegetation. The predominant colours are browns and reds. At this time heather and bracken achieve their full growth and disperse their seeds.

Comparing the earth to language the poet likens the bog to the vowels in its alphabet. The origin of language is submerged like the roots of plants that remain hidden through the seasons. The surface of the language changes just as the plants do with the climate. It absorbs the impression of chance events just as a fruit blown to the ground will merge with the earth.

The poet has been nourished by this figurative soil and, like the willow tree, he returns to it for stability. Next he sees a disused turf cart, its handmade wheels jammed in the decaying surface of the bog. The back of the cart is shaped like a 'cupid's bow' and the sides are like lips. The man who drove the cart was regarded as a god, distributing fuel to the householders. As a boy the poet would bring him food and drink and sometimes ride in the cart like a medieval squire ministering to his knight.

When they passed the women returning from the harvest fields they were greeted and the way was cleared for them. The poet invites us to watch them going through country lanes and to see how he expands with pride when the older man addresses him.

In the final section Tacitus (55–120 AD), the Roman historian of the Germanic tribes, is called upon. The poet asks him to bear witness as he builds an altar on his island which is heaped with corpses. The poet's island does not resemble the one where the goddess of the Germanic people was worshipped. The peace found here is not a comforting one. The land has suffered too many deaths. The buried ones are not at rest for they are watched by soldiers.

Tacitus is asked to be an impartial observer of the poet's society and to examine the bodies of those killed in the present conflict. The historian can then record the sectarian cruelty inflicted in the name of the community, and how it drains the people of all feeling.

COMMENTARY: Memory, for Heaney, is an instinct. As such it is allied to his language, and the rediscovery of his physical origins is combined with the recovery of his linguistic origins. This search is summarised by the incongruous use of the word 'sounded' at the end of Part I where the pools are:

> not to be sounded
> by the naked eye

The notion of 'sounding' has a particular significance for Heaney. Introducing an anthology entitled *Soundings* he wrote of

> an attempt to make poetry once again an act of faith in the land and language that the poet shares with his dead.*

The bog has become a symbol for that dual source. Through it he pursues his 'attempt'. He reads a sacred code in the stacked turf, and the ground emits a noise that is half animal, half human, 'cheeping' like a bird and 'lisping' like a child. When the poet removes the spade in Part III it opens like 'lips' and a muttering sound is produced.

Against the various English words for a marshy place in Part II he sets the Irish word 'bog', its sound expressing more accurately the nature of the bog. Ultimately this leads him to find the vowel sounds in his language at the centre of the bog.

The female associations of the bog, 'insatiable bride', 'bag of waters', 'mothers of autumn', are transferred to the 'vowel'. This connection is a potent one, for Heaney has written elsewhere of vowels as having a feminine quality and this he links in turn with the Irish element in his language.

This heritage has been mother to his poetic growth, establishing the 'nesting ground/outback of my mind' described at the end of Part II. He acknowledges it again in the final verse of Part IV. The word 'Ruminant' at line 33 anticipates this eventual comparison with his mind, for although the literal meaning of the word refers to animals like cows that regurgitate their food it has another sense that refers to deep thought. Its application here harks back to the 'cud of memory' in 'Funeral Rites'. In this deepest recess of memory impressions are stored like eggs waiting to be hatched.

Throughout Part II this preservative function of the bog is portrayed by a series of kennings such as 'Earth-pantry, bone-vault'. The use of this Anglo-Saxon device reveals the other half of the poet's linguistic and racial origins. These figurative parents are represented in Part III by the spade, the man's implement, and by the cloven stick, emblem of the goddess. The spade recalls too the initial image of 'Digging' and thus alludes to the poet's pen. In Part IV it is the root of his language that is preserved by the bog.

Literary tradition is cited here too. The opening line of Part IV: 'This centre holds' is Heaney's response to W.B. Yeats's assertion that 'the centre cannot hold' in his poem 'The Second Coming'. For Seamus Heaney the bog provides the adequate symbol to set against the disorder of his society.

By invoking Tacitus in Part VI, however, he is admitting his own

---

* *Soundings*, Blackstaff, Belfast, 1972.

inability to be an impartial observer of the events that surround him. As in 'Punishment' he is self-accusing but here the implication is more brutal. He employs the terrible force of the word 'slaughter' in a communal admission of complicity with those who kill.

Pagan rituals are alluded to again in this poem. Beginning with the 'hieroglyphic' signs formed by the turf stacks the ceremony proceeds through the 'votive goods' hoarded in Part II to the emergence of the goddess in the next part. In Part V the man who delivers the turf is 'deified' like the Tollund man. Christian and pagan terms are mixed in the final section. At the centre of the 'mother ground' is a 'sacred heart'. The latter phrase is used in the Catholic church to denote a manifestation of Jesus Christ. Juxtaposed with this is the quotation from Tacitus's *Germania** where the sacred grove of the goddess is located on an 'island of the ocean'. It is to this primitive goddess that the poet and his people now do homage.

The narrow verse forms of this poem correspond to its archaeological context. Its shape provides a visual equivalent to that plumbing of a depth implied in 'sounding' and to the process of digging both for turf and for historical artefacts. By using alliteration and kennings the poet sustains the allusion to Anglo-Saxon forms while continuing to describe his Irish origins.

NOTES AND GLOSSARY:

quagmire:	moist boggy ground
morass:	wet ground, a marsh
midden:	a dung heap
cloven oak limb:	divided trunk or branch of an oak tree
felloes:	rims of wheels
cupid's bow:	the small bow from which Cupid shoots his love-darts; woman's lips shaped like a bow
haw-lit:	brightened by the hawthorn berries
crannog:	(*Gaelic*) fortified island in a lake, lake dwelling

---

from **'Singing School'**   *North*

The title of this sequence is taken from a line in W.B. Yeats's poem, 'Sailing to Byzantium'. It documents some of the attitudes and associations that have informed the poet's creative development.

1. 'Ministry of Fear'. This poem is dedicated to Heaney's friend and fellow poet, Seamus Deane (*b*. 1940), now professor of English Literature

---

* *Germania* (AD98) was an account of the beliefs and customs of the Germanic tribes. The description is cast in Roman terms, the local gods being equated with the Roman ones. The particular interest of these tribes lay in the fact that the Romans never succeeded in conquering them.

at University College, Dublin. A quotation from Patrick Kavanagh opens the poem. The facetious remark that they have lived in 'important places' is followed by a description of the poet's first term at St Columb's school in Derry. It was here that he met Seamus Deane who lived nearby.

From the school windows the boy could see across the city to the race track at Brandywell. This was floodlit for the evening greyhound races. He was so depressed at being away from home that he could not eat the biscuits intended to comfort him. He tossed them across the school fence one night. As he did so he saw the gleam of house lights beyond him in the fog. In retrospect he recognises the furtive nature of his deed.

He tells of going from school to university in Belfast and then to Berkeley, California. By that time both he and his friend were established poets. They sent letter poems to one another and later sent each other their first published collections with a formal inscription.

It was at school that they had begun this exchange of poems. His friend's verses then had seemed strange to Seamus Heaney. He compares their effects to the twirling seeds of the sycamore tree. Of himself he says that he wrote about trees. His accent could produce unusual rhymes. He pictures this accent as a pair of farmer's boots walking across the garden of standard English.

He wonders if their accents have changed and recalls a theory that the diction of Catholic schoolboys was not as clear as that of their Protestant counterparts. It was a comment designed to breed in them a feeling of inferiority.

The priest would make him repeat his name in order to test his pronunciation. Corporal punishment at school was meted out with a leather strap but the boy never wrote about his fear of this in letters to his parents. Now the poet chides himself for his reluctance to speak up.

Driving home one summer evening after his first romantic encounter with a girl he was halted by a police roadblock. As the police gathered around the car one pointed a gun at him and asked his name. His Irish first name revealed his background and allegiances. At another roadblock the police read his letters and tried to decipher one from Seamus Deane.

The poem concludes with the assertion that although Ulster is ruled from England, English poetry is not the exclusive property of that country. This is the first breaking of the silence with which he and his friend had reacted to the intimidation within their society.

2. **'A Constable Calls'.** From a boy's eye-view the poet observes a policeman who has come to record details of the crops grown and harvested on the farm.

The policeman's bicycle stands outside the window in the sun. The boy enumerates its polished protective fittings. His eye travels then to the policeman's hat lying upside down beside his feet. He notices the sloping mark left on the man's hair by the rim of his hat.

The policeman writes down the details given by the boy's father in a large accounts book. The father recites the list, giving the area of land sown with each particular crop. The atmosphere is tense and the boy fixes his eyes on the gun and holster at the policeman's waist.

The farmer is questioned to ensure that nothing has been omitted from the list. When he replied that it is complete the boy feels guilty on his behalf, knowing that there is a row of turnips at the end of the potato field. He envisages the jail in the barracks as a dungeon.

When the policeman stands up to go the boy notices the baton case hanging at his side. Before he leaves the policeman glances at the boy and replaces his hat. Fixing the ledger to his back-carrier he cycles away. The boy hears the ticking of the bicycle chain.

5. 'Fosterage'. Like 'The Ministry of Fear' this poem is dedicated to a friend and fellow writer, Michael McLaverty.*

The short story writer gives advice to the young poet. He stresses the importance of accurate description, quoting Katherine Mansfield's† words about reporting detail. To balance this advice he warns the poet against overwriting and refers to the energetic language of Hopkins.

The poet still has a copy of Hopkins's *Journals* given to him by his friend. It has been underlined in places showing how Hopkins curbed his energy. This underlining reveals, too, something of Michael McLaverty's character in his awareness of the quality of patience. The poet recalls the older man's paternal interest and encouragement.

6. 'Exposure'. This final part of 'Singing School' is the last poem in *North* and describes the poet's removal from Belfast to County Wicklow.

The countryside is bleak with the rain and the pale light of winter. The poet is waiting to see a comet predicted for this day. He imagines that it will come in a flush of reds like the berries on the hedges. Occasionally he sees falling stars and thinks of the excitement he would feel

---

* Michael McLaverty: born in 1907 in County Monaghan, he studied in Belfast and London and returned to teach in Belfast. He was headmaster at St Joseph's College where Seamus Heaney taught for a time. He has written eight novels and several short stories. Heaney wrote an Introduction to McLaverty's *Collected Short Stories* (1978).

† Katherine Mansfield (1888–1923) was born in New Zealand and moved to England in order to pursue a career in writing. Although chiefly known as a short story writer she was a prolific correspondent and journal writer. The quotation in 'Fosterage' is taken from *The Journal of Katherine Mansfield*, ed. John Middleton Murry, Constable & Co. Ltd., London, 1927, p.42. Under the heading 'The Decision' it refers to her resolution to be more precise in her writing style.

at finding a piece of meteorite. The lanes he walks on are covered with the fallen leaves and nuts and shells of autumn.

He compares himself to a warrior in a primitive arena wasting his talent in a futile effort to relieve a despairing community. He wonders what has brought him to this point and considers the reasonable advice of his friends and the bitterness of his enemies.

In this internal debate he balances the burden of his responsibilities and his regrets. He questions his reasons for writing, whether it is for his own pleasure, or for the public, or as a response to those who criticise him. The sound of rain is to him like low voices talking of disappointment and the loss of certainty. The individual drops, however, remind him of enduring truth.

He defines himself by stating that he is not an imprisoned rebel, nor is he a traitor. He has migrated inwards, becoming introspective, concealed like the rebels of the sixteenth century who took refuge in the woods. Having fled the battlefield he remains on its perimeter, disguised and protected by the trees, alert to every change in the wind.

This attention to his own needs has distracted him from the arrival of the anticipated comet and he has not seen its exotic light.

COMMENTARY: In *North* 'Singing School' is prefaced by quotations from Yeats and Wordsworth. In these extracts both poets refer to formative influences on their poetry. Through his sequence Seamus Heaney likewise identifies literary, political and personal factors that have motivated his writing.

Repression and subterfuge are the first of these experiences to be described. Figures of authority, the priest and the police in the opening poems, become agents of repression. When he arrives as a boarder at the school he regards himself as a soldier lodged or 'billeted' in a barracks. The school itself is isolated, set apart from the town on a hill. The environment menaces the boy; its dogtrack is like a diseased throat choked by the electric hare. His loneliness is emphasised by the sight of the house lights seen gleaming through the school fence.

Early in his life the poet learns the self-protective art of subterfuge and silence as he flings the biscuits over the fence at night and does not tell of the beatings in the headmaster's study. He remains mute, too, in 'A Constable Calls', aware though he is of his father's guilt. His ultimate silence is in the tacit recognition shared by his friend of the subtle process of intimidation operating in their society. Set against his reticence is the first awareness of language as a political indicator in names and accents. He rejects the English pronunciation of 'pushed' and 'pulled', keeping his local accent. His name is twice interpreted as a declaration of his creed and background. The language of poetry remains mysterious, resisting especially the prying curiosity of the police at the roadblocks. His friend's 'hieroglyphics', recalling those in 'Kinship', are like a secret code.

The voices of other poets are heard in 'The Ministry of Fear'. The quotation in the opening lines is from Patrick Kavanagh's poem 'Epic'. At line 35 the phrase 'stuff as dreams are made on' is an oblique reference to Prospero's words in Shakespeare's *The Tempest*, IV.1.155–6: 'We are such stuff/As dreams are made on, and our little life/Is rounded with a sleep.' The poem shares its title with Graham Greene's (*b*. 1904) novel (Greene himself has said that he took the title from a poem by Wordsworth). Humorously alluding to the youthful earnestness of himself and Seamus Deane, Heaney varies a line from Shakespeare's *King Lear*, III.4.104, saying 'Here's two on's are sophisticated'. The only freedom mentioned is in his friend's poetry, an abandon that goes undetected by the police.

Similar in form and location to 'Mossbawn: 1. Sunlight', Part 2 of this sequence is filled with a presence very different from that of the earlier poem. There are few images to relieve the catalogue of the policeman's effects. The boy's attention shifts from the details of the policeman's bicycle to the imposing bulk of the policeman himself. His feet weigh heavy on the pedal treads and his hat is tight on his head, the ledger is strapped down, the holster buttoned and tied.

Fear sharpens the boy's senses and he takes in all those things associated with the constable in clear detail. Each sentence is a statement of fact. 'The boot of the law' is a phrase that plays on the colloquial expression 'the arm of the law' and its more threatening force pervades the poem. In the final verse it is this boot, not the constable's foot, that sets the bicycle in motion. As it moves away its tick has the menacing insistence of an explosive timing device, a sound that reinforces the contrast with 'Sunlight' where the only sound was the ticking of the clocks.

Hopkins was one of the poets whose work first influenced Heaney and it is appropriate that he should be included in Part 5, 'Fosterage', as one of the masters of the 'Singing School'. He is mentioned through the words of Michael McLaverty. This man imposes a new duty on Heaney to be a serious poet. Where first language was enjoyed for its own sake as the poet was 'cubbed' in it, now words will be 'obols', the pennies used to close the eyes of the dead.

Here, as in 'The Ministry of Fear', Heaney combines the ordinary phrases of conversation with literary quotation. The informal movement of 'Fosterage' is tightened by the cross-reference from 'underlined' to 'lineaments' and the allusion to Hopkins's poem 'The Windhover' in the word 'buckled'. The colloquial sound of the lines:

But to hell with overstating it:
'Don't have the veins bulging in your biro.'

is countered by the serious note of the final lines and the alliterating archaic words 'obeisant' and 'obols'. These combine to express the poet's new sense of discipline and awe in regard to his poetry.

Katherine Mansfield's 'exile' and Michael McLaverty's exhortation to 'do your own thing' are recalled by the poet now that he has turned to writing as a career.

His 'exile' becomes an 'exposure' in the final part of the sequence. The sense of finality signalled by the close of the day and the ending of the year oppresses the poet. His isolation is intensified by this dismal weather and the only relief he anticipates is the brief light of a comet. Autumn decay which was evoked by the 'ferments of husk and leaf' in 'Kinship' IV is continued here but the maternal aspect of the process is missing:

> Instead I walk through damp leaves
> Husks, the spent flukes of autumn.

The poet now identifies himself with the trees, an image that recalls the description of his poetry in the first part of this sequence.

At a reading Heaney explained that this poem works on three levels. The title refers to media exposure, exposure to the elements and exposure of the self through poetry. Up to this point his poems have been presented through personae reflecting aspects of himself, for example, the young boy in the early poems or the women in *Door into the Dark* and *Wintering Out*. 'Singing School' is distinguished from these poems by the poet's desire to speak with a natural autobiographical voice.

The exposure through exile is a continuation of those other quests into the self undertaken at the end of the previous collections. Media exposure has forced the poet to be a spokesman for the minority community in the North of Ireland. When he leaves that place he is accused of a betrayal, hence the defensive tone of the eighth verse.

Yeatsian tones and syntax have entered the poem at the fifth verse with the lines:

> I often think of my friends'
> Beautiful prismatic counselling
> And the anvil brains of some who hate me

Heaney is confronted by a dilemma similar to that experienced by his predecessor. Caught in the middle of a civil war he wonders should he write or act, and, if he writes, how can he justify his doing so. These are the responsibilities that burden him in the next verse.

The disillusionment and the loss of values brought about by war are expressed by the rain. Beyond this, however, Heaney perceives an abiding truth and chooses in the end to be faithful to his art even if it produces only 'sparks' and not the flare of the comet. He is reduced to a primitive condition looking inwards rather than responding to the expectations of his audience.

The loose forms and abundant dialogue of the poems in 'Singing School' represent the poet's need to expand the range of his voice again after the constricted forms of the first part of *North*. The silence of guilt broken in those poems is paralleled in the 'Singing School' by a defensive silence. He follows the example of other writers and obeys his own poetic inclinations regardless of whether or not it is considered cowardly of him to leave the field of battle.

Part 3

Commentary

SEAMUS HEANEY BELIEVES IN THE spiritual power of poetry as being necessary to the survival of the community. He has declared this belief in the form of an act of faith:

> I assume that to be able to make his personal cry resonant for his generation and the generations that succeed him, the poet will have to be gifted with an ear that is deeply tuned to the genius of his language. I assume that poetic craft and technique, once they have been learned will disappear into the voice and appear as sureness of tone from poem to poem and that there will always be a nicely held tension between poetry's need to be true to the impurities of life and its need to remember that it intends to be pure language.*

Through the work included in the *Selected Poems* this assimilation of technical skills by the poet's voice can be observed. The short lyrics of Heaney's first collection give way to the systained series and sequences of the later ones. Consistent with this development is the gradual concentration of the poet's focus on particular themes.

Themes

History

Irish history, as it was taught to Seamus Heaney at school, stopped at the end of the nineteenth century. The first of his historical poems are 'At a Potato Digging' and 'Requiem for the Croppies'. The former refers to the potato famine of 1845–8 and the second to an incident in the 1798 rebellion. These poems are significant not only because they reflect the emotive influence still exerted by these events but because of the final images presented by the poet.

In 'At a Potato Digging' the time-scale shifts from the present to the past and back again to the present. Part IV concludes with a picture of the labourers throwing their scraps on the ground like an offering to the earth goddess mentioned in Part I. This continuing automatic

* 'Current Unstated Assumptions about Poetry', *Critical Inquiry*, 7, 4, 1981.

homage to an ancient deity reveals their profound fear of a recurrence of the famine.

The implications of the crop of barley at the end of 'Requiem for the Croppies' matter more to the poet than the date or location of the battle. That crop anticipated the possible realisation of the croppies' dream that was to be effected by further rebellions. This theme is reiterated in the linguistic image of 'A New Song' and in the malevolent child in 'Act of Union'.

History in these poems is fused with the poet's knowledge of the natural environment and the cycles of the farming year. Like the seasons it is seen to move through a cyclical course.

When the poet observes his countryside in 'Bogland' and in *Wintering Out* he discerns in its contours and landmarks evidence of its history. Language too bears the imprint of the past, as is shown in the poem 'Traditions'. Images of a primeval world occur naturally to Seamus Heaney, for example the 'millions of years' recorded in the depth of the bog in 'Bogland' or the signs of a primitive battle imagined in 'The Wife's Tale'. The place-name poems of *Wintering Out* testify, too, to this fascination with the earliest phases of social development and of language.

Primed thus by a cyclical view of history and by a preference for images of an elemental type, Heaney's imagination was alert to the symbolic possibilities of the bog bodies as photographed and described in P.V. Glob's text. In 'The Tollund Man', the first of the poems inspired by Glob's work, the poet suggests a connection between these sacrificial victims and the contemporary victims of sectarian violence. The incident cited in the second part of the poem occurred some years before the present conflict but its motive has not changed.

The poetic sensibility in the first half of *North* is dominated by the bog bodies and their historical context. Through them the poet is able to observe the history being made in his world today. He is forced to acknowledge too that acts of violence represent the continuity of a pre-rational impulse in the same way as rudimentary forms of speech have survived in his language. By calling on Tacitus in 'Kinship' he asserts the need for a poet to take on some of the duties of the historian.

History, then, in Heaney's poetry is not seen as a simple documentation of salient facts in a nation's development, but as a potent force that moulds both a nation's view of itself and an individual's self-image. The encounter with the bog bodies touched an intensely personal area within the poet's imagination and connected at the same time with the public events in his society. In the autobiographical poems at the end of *North* he moves towards the proposition that the history of a people is contained in the life of the individual. This perception is likewise the basis for his first historical poems.

Ritual and tradition

In the opening poem of *Death of a Naturalist* Heaney describes the tradition he was expected to follow. As a compromise between this expectation and his own inclination he imagines his pen to be a spade. Other forms of the traditional activities pursued in the countryside where he grew up are the subject of poems such as 'Churning Day'; 'Follower'; 'The Diviner'; 'The Forge'; 'A Lough Neagh Sequence' and 'Mossbawn'. In each of these the poet observes the manual skills that sustained the farming community.

He sees the people handling their tools with an unconscious familiarity, and, as an onlooker, he is aware of some invisible power being summoned through their work. In his descriptions the poet surrounds these tasks with a religious aura. The anvil of the blacksmith is an 'altar'. The diggers and the fishermen regard the earth and the lake with awe. Their skill has been passed on by a previous generation and in this way tradition represents an active bond with the past.

As these tasks harmonise with the seasons, so religious ritual parallels organic process. In 'Funeral Rites' the bodies of the dead are embalmed and purified and in 'Kinship' it is the bog that accomplishes this transformation, when the poet addresses it as

... enbalmer
of votive goods
and sabred fugitives.

The faces of the poet's dead relatives in 'Funeral Rites' are 'soapstone masks' but the bodies preserved in the bog revert to an organic state.

In 'Summer Home' the poet tries to heal the pain that he has brought upon his wife by ritual gestures, making the flowers a 'may altar' and their scent a 'chrism' to 'anoint' the metaphorical wound.

The wondering respect with which the boy watched the manual work on the farm is magnified in the poet's confrontation with the Tollund man. He has said that on writing this poem he was struck by a sense of fear and describes the poem as a vow 'to pray to the Tollund Man and assist at his enshrined head'.* By this vow Heaney makes his poem into a prayer or sacred promise. Praying to a pagan god he transgresses the Christian code. Later, in 'Westering' he blasphemes again by travelling on a Good Friday.

He proceeds in the first part of *North* to establish an alternative ritual to the Christian one portrayed in 'Funeral Rites', I. The subsequent poems are imbued with the reverent tone that characterised the opening of 'The Tollund Man'. The deliberate naming of each part of

* 'Feeling into Words', *Preoccupations*, p.59.

the preserved bodies renders their image solid in the reader's mind and produces a contemplative rhythm inviting the reader to worship them too. In contrast, however, the poet introduces the crudely murdered bodies of the present. Although these deaths testify to the survival of an ancient instinct no corresponding tradition remains to remove the traces of their pain or to assimilate the grief of the community.

In 'Kinship' the poet invokes the 'sacred heart' of the earth goddess, again employing a Christian idiom in a pagan context. The association of the bog and the language made through this poem extends the power of the goddess and establishes her as the poet's muse. From this point on his poetry includes a range of allusions to his literary antecedents thus asserting the tradition in which he has chosen to follow.

Language

From the title poem of his first collection, language is a constant subject of Heaney's poetry. Only after he has learnt the meaning of the word 'frogspawn' and been told that the bullfrogs 'croak', does the boy come to fear the frogs.

Door into the Dark, the title of Seamus Heaney's second collection, is described by the poet as referring to an entry into language:

> Words themselves are doors, Janus is to a certain extent their deity, looking back to a ramification of roots and associations and forward to a clarification of sense and meaning.*

This progression continues from the final line of 'Personal Helicon' at the end of *Death of a Naturalist*. There the young boy's habit of peering into wells is transformed into the young man's interest in writing poetry. Water also forms the basis of the linguistic association that prompts 'Undine'. With its echo of the Latin word 'unda' for a wave this word is the starting point for Heaney's reworking of the old tale of the water sprite taking a human form.

Through the poems of *Wintering Out* the poet approaches the political tensions of his native place from the perspective of his dialect. In 'Bog Oak' and 'Traditions' he sets the standard English modes of speech against the local Hiberno-English ones. He demonstrates the idiosyncracy of this deviant language in its preservation of seventeenth-century English forms and of Old Norse words introduced by the Scottish settlers. Despite this diversity he finds in the language a unity sufficient to give coherence to the idea of a nation. Quoting James Joyce, the poet formulates a response to the English notion of the Irish as expressed by Spenser and Shakespeare.

---

* *Poetry Book Society Bulletin*, 61, 1969.

'Anahorish', 'Broagh' and 'A New Song' establish an area within the poet's language that is specifically Irish and has a subversive force. Each of the names is associated with water and in 'A New Song' the poet incites the river Moyola to swell its banks and lay claim to the land. This undercurrent in the Irish language is further embodied in the shadowy figures that people the poems of *Wintering Out*. Their exclusion from human company corresponds to the repression of the Irish language.

By rediscovering the 'roots' of his language Seamus Heaney effects that 'clarification of sense and meaning' anticipated in the nature of words. The bog that was memory in 'Bogland' speaks now in an ancient half-forgotten language, presented through 'hieroglyphs' and in its cheeping, lisping and muttering in 'Kinship'. Just as butter and bodies are preserved in the bog so the persistence of its Irish name points to the conservation of an Irish element within the English language. Through these poems Seamus Heaney overcomes silence. In 'Punishment' it is the silence of guilt and complicity and in 'Singing School' it is the silence of resistance. The sectarian bias attached to accent and name in 'The Ministry of Fear' is refuted by the poet's statement that:

> Ulster was British, but with no rights on
> The English lyric . . .

The poet has established that English is his language too, albeit an English varied by the regional imprint of an Irish idiom. Like the bog it has preservative and generative properties.

The centre of the bog in 'Kinship' IV is equivalent to vowel sounds and out of their interaction with other features of the language the poet has grown. The potential to 'clarify' inherent in the nature of words is fulfilled by poetry.

Imagery

In his first poems Seamus Heaney returns to the life of the farm where he grew up. As he is perceiving that life from the point of view of a child his recollections are filtered through his senses. Consequently, the early poems abound in a tactile vocabulary recreating those impressions.

Danger is concealed in the natural order and this is expressed in weapon imagery. The sequence of these images begins in 'Digging' where the pen, the gun and the spade are brought into a parallel relation. The angry bullfrogs in 'Death of a Naturalist' become 'mud grenades'. Similar images pervade the other poems in this first collection, and they recur in certain poems in *Door into the Dark*. The woman in 'The Wife's Tale' imagines the pitchforks to be 'javelins' and the stubble field to be the site of an ancient battle. An actual battle provides the subject for 'Requiem for the Croppies'.

The child's fear and wonder remain with the poet as he grows and in 'Vision' at the end of 'A Lough Neagh Sequence' the imagined rope of lice becomes reality in the form of the eels crossing the grass at night. The menacing forces of the natural world are represented in this second collection by the vague mystery of darkness. This, in its turn, is summarised by the bottomless centre of the bog.

When the poet is subsequently confronted by the bog bodies his fear is renewed and deepened. The images of violence prompted by these bodies are the more frightening for being linked to contemporary events. Momentarily the poet identifies himself with the victims in 'The Tollund Man' and again in 'Punishment'.

A battle is played out between the poet and his wife in 'Summer Home' as their anger is compared to a sword and the pain it causes to a 'wound'. Psychological fear pervades 'Singing School' in the form of authority figures such as schoolmasters and the police. Their power, however, is asserted by actual weapons which prompt a defiant silence in the boy and the poet.

Animal characteristics and maladies are ascribed to the earth and the language. In 'Death of a Naturalist' the countryside is diseased by the rotting flax which 'festered in the heart of the townland'. The potato blight in 'At a Potato Digging' infects the land with a 'running sore'. Even the moon, in 'Westering', is like a skin with 'enlarged pores' and the light it casts is a 'bony shine'. The last traces of the Irish language are described in 'Traditions' as the uvula and the coccyx.

Conversely the bodies taken out of the bog are described in vegetal terms, their features being compared to 'peat', 'pods' and 'amber'. Linguistic images are transferred to the body of the bog in 'Kinship' with references to the 'vowel of the earth', 'mutation' and 'root'. This last is given an ambiguity that combines both its linguistic and its organic meanings.

The theme of ritual is reflected in the recurrent imagery of altars, particularly in 'At a Potato Digging', 'The Forge' and 'Summer Home'. Worship at these altars seeks to appease the unseen forces that impinge on the child's consciousness and, later, on that of the poet.

Symbolism

The titles of Seamus Heaney's first four works are consistent in their negative implications. It would be natural to suppose that their dominant symbols would proceed from the suggestions of death, darkness and the barren cold of winter and northern landscapes. The surrounding context of organic process mitigates this effect. Earth, water, woman and the bog are the chief symbols that provide this balance.

From the initial association of the pen and the spade Heaney equates the earth with his poetic imagination and the roots embedded in that earth represent his own origins. The farming tradition among his people is simultaneously involved with decay and growth. Autumn is the season during which these two processes coincide as the full growth of summer begins to die.

In 'At a Potato Digging' earth is both worshipped and cursed and the continuity of farm labour is likened to the seasonal return of autumn. In 'Kinship' the poet's probing of his past leads him to the 'mothers of autumn' who are both womb and grave. At the end of *North* he wanders in the woods and likens himself to the 'Husks, the spent flukes of autumn'.

The darkness which the poet approaches is this creative source. He invokes it as a divine power and penetrates it by way of ritual and poetry. 'Bogland' is the gathering point for all those intimations of darkness carried through *Death of a Naturalist* and *Door into the Dark*. Its potential as a symbol of the poet's racial memory and creative imagination is fulfilled through the bog bodies. Through his encounter with the Tollund man the poet 'consecrates' the bog and, later, in 'Kinship' he refers to its 'sacred heart'.

The bodies drawn out of the bog are tied to the poet by the lines of physical and linguistic evolution. They symbolise the point at which his heritage of instinctive feeling coincides with his acquired cultural attitudes. Through this association the poet equates the dark female centre of the bog with his subconscious memory, the source of his poetic imagination.

Versification

In his essay on the poetry of Wordsworth and Yeats, Seamus Heaney described the types of sound out of which a poet's voice is formed:

> What kinds of noise assuage him, what kinds of music pleasure or repel him, what messages the receiving stations of his senses are happy to pick up from the world around him and what ones they automatically block out—all this unconscious activity at the pre-verbal level, is entirely relevant to the intonations and appeasements offered by a poet's music.*

Patterns of imitative sounds presented by way of assonance and alliteration characterise the first poems in *Death of a Naturalist*. These sounds correspond to a sensory awareness of the world and set up an internal stress, for example, in 'Digging':

* 'The Makings of a Poet's Music', *Preoccupations*, p.61.

Under my window, a clean rasping sound
When the spade sinks into gravelly ground:
My father, digging. I look down.

Here the striking of the spade into the earth is imitated by the sibilant extension of 'rasping' in 'spade', 'sound' and 'sinks', and the sudden halting of the sequence in the guttural alliteration of 'gravelly ground' and the double 'g' of 'digging'. The rhyme of 'sound' and 'ground' amplifies the effect of the spade delving into the soil.

Similar patterns can be discerned in 'Death of a Naturalist'. Notice in particular the use of imitative words such as 'slap', 'squelch', 'plop' and 'croak' and the echo of their sounds. Internal rhyme is used more frequently than end-rhyme in these early collections. The rhyming couplets of 'At a Potato Digging' II are an exception to this and their rhymes are at times somewhat forced in their effect.

Chief among the natural sounds that influence the poet's voice are the cadences of speech and dialect, and ultimately these dictate the rhythm of the poem. Colloquial expressions are interjected as in 'Digging' and 'A Lough Neagh Sequence' or else they are directly quoted, as in 'The Wife's Tale' and 'Singing School'.

The flexibility of the verse forms makes possible the inclusion of these direct quotations. The strict classical form of the sonnet is used only twice, in 'The Forge' and in 'Mossbawn 2. The Seed Cutters'.

Imitative forms are preferred by the poet as in 'Sargasso' and 'The Return' from 'A Lough Neagh Sequence' which emulate the sinuous shape of the eels, and the careful movements needed to catch the worms are portrayed by the rhyme scheme of 'Bait'. The distinctive narrow verse forms of the bog poems in the first part of *North* represent the layered depths of the bog.

In these poems Heaney employs certain devices of Anglo-Saxon poetry, in particular the kennings and the double alliteration. Stress in Old English poetry fell on alliterating words. In 'Punishment' the first double alliteration is repeated: 'halter at the nape', 'her neck', 'her naked', her nipples', and further down, again, in close proximity are 'barked sapling', 'stubble of black', 'soiled bandage'. There are no end-rhymes and the rhythm of the poem depends on these internal features.

The almost equal stress thus laid on monosyllabic words causes the polysyllabic ones to be aurally divided too, so that both syllables of 'blindfold' and 'bandage' are emphasised. The lines are short, varying from a basic quantity of five syllables. In contrast to the tight structure of these poems the final ones of *North*, represented here by 'Singing School', are free-ranging in their form, and reflect the ppoet's desire to find a new voice after the refined structures of the bog poems.

Diction

The vocabulary of Seamus Heaney's early poems is predominantly tactile. The awakening of the poet's perceptive faculties is expressed by details of sensory impressions. Potatoes are remembered for their 'cool hardness' in 'Digging' and for their 'solid feel' in 'At a Potato Digging', seed in 'The Wife's Tale' is 'innumerable and cool'. Throughout these poems verbs of natural processes, of decay and growth, interact with concrete nouns. The natural world is an extension of the poet's self. Memories remain with him as 'living roots'. In 'Kinship' he compares himself to a weeping willow leaning into the ground.

This ground is language. As the poet progresses his diction is expanded by the acquisition of a technical vocabulary drawn from the sciences of anatomy, archaeology and linguistics. All are defined within a natural context, the landscape is endowed with a linguistic character, and in 'Traditions' language is given a human body complete with uvula and coccyx. The bog becomes a stomach, a womb and a grave, performing all those processes of nourishment and decay described in the preceding poems.

Seamus Heaney is not concerned simply to reproduce physical sensation through language but is intent on revealing the actual origin of words and language. Thus, the poem 'Undine' is developed from the etymology of the word. In 'Broagh' the constituents of the word are examined in relation to the place they name. The final 'gh' is evidence of the 'guttural muse' whose neglect is described in 'Traditions'. So too is the word 'bog', the sound of which resonates through 'Kinship' II, where it is fused with archaic English forms.

The poet's appreciation of the cadence and forms of his dialect is further reflected by his use of proverbs as in 'Digging' and 'A Lough Neagh Sequence', and by the direct speech in, for example, 'The Wife's Tale' and 'Singing School'. His syntax too is governed by a conversational directness and the poems build from a muted opening line such as 'We have no prairies' in 'Bogland' or 'Some day I will go to Aarhus' in 'The Tollund Man'.

Occasionally French words, such as 'cortège' and 'boulevard' in 'Funeral Rites' and 'voyeur' in 'Punishment', vary the Anglo-Saxon concentration of Seamus Heaney's vocabulary. Abstract Latinate words are deployed more frequently in the later poems. Balanced by the effect of assonance and alliteration they are given a concrete weight within the physical context of the poems, as with the phrase 'connive/in civilised outrage' in 'Punishment' and the lines

the cud of memory
allayed for once, arbitration
of the feud placated.

from 'Funeral Rites'. By this combination of abstract state and the physical fact (the 'cud' and the 'feud'), and by his consistent rhythmical arrangement of dialect words and speech patterns, Heaney confirms his belief that the 'impurities of life' can be presented by the 'purities' of language.

Part 4

Hints for study

General

Before studying the *Selected Poems* of Seamus Heaney read them
through at least once for pleasure. Although the text consists of poems
extracted from four collections there is continuity within the selection
and it is well to be familiar with all its contents. For your purposes,
however, it may be better to study a few poems in detail at first rather
than to acquire a cursory knowledge of all of them.

Some of the most significant poems have been discussed in Part 3
above. This analysis can serve as a guideline for your own study. If you
are concentrating only on a few poems you should choose a sample
from each of the collections represented here. In this way the possibili-
ties for comparison and study of the poet's development are extended.

From your initial reading you will have gleaned something of the
poet's major concerns, for example by observing the recurrence of cer-
tain subjects and images. Now, when you return to the individual
poems, all your critical faculties should be alert.

It is essential first to understand the primary meaning of the poem,
to have its images clear in your mind. Two, and sometimes three or
four, readings are necessary before this is achieved. Allow some time to
elapse between these readings. If a poem proves too difficult at first,
set it aside for a while. Some new aspect will present itself when you
next read the poem.

An examination of the diction and devices of the poem will open its
meaning even further. Determine first who is the persona speaking
through the poem. Is it a child, a lover, a woman, a traveller, a poet?
Does the poem establish a particular location or generate an atmos-
phere or mood? Once these aspects have been identified you should
then note the imagery that contributes to this physical context. Pick
out the other features of presentation such as the figurative structures
of metaphor, simile, symbol or personification. Decide how these
work in extending the scope of the theme.

Within the compressed format of a poem every word is vital. The
vocabulary operates at different levels, each corresponding to an
amplification of the poet's meaning. Mark any words that recur. What
bearing does this repetition have on the progress and sense of the poem
and to what extent is the sense of the repeated words altered if at all?

Read the poems aloud to get the full effect of alliteration, assonance, onomatopoeia and rhyme employed by the poet.

Is the vocabulary unusual in any way? Does it contain foreign words or technical terms, slang or dialect? Consider the function of these words in relation to the rest of the vocabulary. Trace the significance of any allusions the poet makes to mythology, history, literature or religion. Gauge the poet's tone by his attitude to his subject and to his reader. To what extent does he manipulate a reader's response to the poem?

When you have noted down these various points and any unusual features of the poem that have struck you, assess its relation to the other poems in the volume. Draw comparisons or contrasts with those other poems you have chosen to study. Determine the general qualities of the poet's style, his approach to specific themes, his preference for particular types of words and images. Trace the signs of his development in respect of each of these characteristics.

Form and prosody are always contentious matters in the discussion of poetry. The shape of a poem, whether a sonnet, an ode, an elegy or free verse should be apparent straightaway. Within these frames, then, a certain metre will be anticipated such as the iambic pentameter in the case of a sonnet. What gives the poem its individual character is the particular variation the poet has wrought on this scheme. The basic rhythm is always determined by the intonations of natural speech. The juxtaposition of words through a rhyme can affect the meaning of those words.

Having thus formed your own view of the poems turn to some of the critical texts (see Part 5 below). It is always best to wait until after you have spent some time on the study of the work yourself before reading the comments of other critics. These comments, when you do come to them, may confirm some of your own ideas as well as proposing new points to observe in the work. They are not the final word and should not be considered as such. There is no definitive interpretation or explanation of a poem. This is one of the pleasures of studying literature, namely, that there is always the possibility of discovering something fresh. Critical texts provide a helpful example of the method and the vocabulary employed in literary interpretation.

The most effective way to organise your notes and ideas is to write an essay. Suggested headings are given in the form of sample questions below. In writing these essays you should use appropriate quotations to support your points. These should be chosen for their relevance to the poet's theme and as examples of the poet's figurative or rhetorical devices. The essays will be of benefit when the time comes to revise your work for examinations.

Group study

This can be a useful exercise, particularly in the case of poetry. A small group of three to five people is preferable in order to allow everyone a chance to speak. Decide beforehand what poem or poems you wish to study and choose one person to read aloud. This will help you to appreciate the aural effects of the piece, in particular the way in which a line break or a division into verses can be elided by the logic of a sentence or the movement of a rhythm. Your ear will be drawn to the projection of certain words through rhetorical devices such as onomatopoeia and rhyme.

If each member of the group has prepared a different aspect of the poem, for example, theme, or imagery, diction or metre, these Notes can provide the basis for a discussion of your various ideas about the poem.

Study for an examination

As in every subject preparation is the key to success in an examination. If you have followed the guidelines suggested above your basic work is already done. Setting your sights on the examination will require you to revise your own working notes and essays. Now you should prepare some new essays or at least write down the headings for a particular topic, such as those set out in the questions below.

The procedure for answering an examination question involves three stages. Read the question twice. Prepare your answer on a separate page by noting the essential points in the question and listing below them the main points that occur to you in response. Organise these points into a logical sequence for your argument. If you submit your work sheet with your answer the examiner will be able to see the extent of your preparation and the method behind your answer.

Write your answer. This should be threefold, consisting of an introduction in which you set out the proposition, that is, the basis of your answer. The main text of your answer will be the development of this proposition. New points should be separated into new paragraphs and each point should be substantiated by relevant quotation. The conclusion should reiterate the essential points you have made and emphasise the central point. Keep the terms of the question to the front of your mind and avoid digression.

The examiner wants to ascertain that you are familiar with the work under study and that you have formed your own impression of this work. Every examiner can detect established critical theories. If you must have recourse to a critic then cite his or her name and your source. Do not appropriate another person's theory to use as your own.

You will be expected to include some quotations, but make sure these are to the point and do not tailor your answer to include the only lines you know.

A simple device for keeping your answer clear and accurate is to imagine that you are addressing a person who knows nothing about the topic being discussed. If the ideas are clear in your own mind then they will be clear to the reader.

Be sure to divide the time allotted for the paper by the number of questions to be answered and attempt all the questions that you are supposed to answer even if it means leaving some essays unfinished. It is better to leave some answers incomplete than not to have attempted all of them. When allotting time remember to allow some time for rereading your answers and, where necessary, revising them.

If you have prepared yourself well by studying an adequate number of poems and writing sample essays there is no reason why you should not enjoy the challenge of the examination. A positive attitude can dissolve many of the difficulties.

Sample questions

(1) Take any two of Heaney's poems (from different collections) and compare them for treatment of theme and style, noting signs of the poet's development.

(2) What significance does the title *North* have in respect of the poems in Heaney's fourth collection?

(3) Assess Heaney's view of time and history.

(4) Heaney has said of his first four collections that they are 'one book'. What evidence can you find to support this idea?

(5) Examine the role of landscape in Heaney's poems.

(6) What significance does the old way of life and manual work in the countryside have for Heaney as a poet?

(7) Discuss the tension between the primitive and the civilised modes of perception as represented in Heaney's poetry.

(8) Consider the work of Heaney in relation to that of any other twentieth-century poet in your course.

(9) The word 'growth' occurs frequently in Heaney's poetic criticism. Has this concept any application to his own work?

(10) Choose two of the following topics and describe Heaney's treatment of them on the basis of his *Selected Poems 1965–1975*: (*a*) love; (*b*) death; (*c*) faith; (*d*) fear.

(11) Discuss the use of colloquial diction in Heaney's *Selected Poems*.

(12) Compare the function and effect of the female voice in 'Undine' and 'The Wife's Tale'.

Some suggested answers

(2) What significance does the title *North* have in respect of the poems in Heaney's fourth collection?

OUTLINE:

North—significance—associations?

(a) Geographical: polar North: cold/barren
                          Northern Europe
                          Northern Ireland/poet's birthplace

(b) Historical: invasion of Ireland by Vikings.
                          The Bog People: bodies in Danish and Irish bogs: similar rituals: worship of a similar deity

(c) Cultural: Anglo-Saxon origin of English language
                          Introduction of English into Ireland
                          Germanic literature: celebration of heroic code: honour and revenge

(d) Political: English sovereignty over Northern Ireland
                          Contemporary conflict

ANSWER:

For Seamus Heaney 'north' is a geographical point with personal and racial associations. In the North of Ireland he was born and much of his inherited culture is derived from the influence of the Vikings, English and Scots who settled at different times in that region. The English language is his first language. Against the frozen, barren implications of a polar north Seamus Heaney sets the soft fertility of the bog, a landscape common to his country and to the countries of northern Europe. It is the landscape in which he grew up.

The opening poems in *North* are named after the poet's home farm, Mossbawn. In these he describes the timeless tranquillity of farm work; the woman in the kitchen in 'Sunlight' bakes scones to the 'tick of two clocks'. The 'seed cutters' in Part 2 work with a deliberate slowness, perpetuating the 'calendar customs' that mark the routines of farm work.

In 'Funeral Rites' the poet steps outside his home, imagining a ritual journey that will pass through 'Strang and Carling fjords'. These are lakeside towns founded by the Viking settlers; their names are today altered to Strangford and Carlingford, but here the poet reverts to the archaic form in keeping with the ancient ceremony he revives. 'Kinship', too, is a linguistic exploration of the place in which the poet asserts the fundamental Irishness of the bog, the word and its meaning untranslatable into modern English. The only effective translation is

made through the use of a series of 'kennings', an Anglo-Saxon poetic
device: 'Earth-pantry, bone-vault, sun-bank'. The autobiographical
poems in the sequence 'Singing School' trace the poet's education in
Derry and Belfast and finally his migration to the South of Ireland.

These poems are coloured by another association linked with the
word north, namely the conflict within the political entity of Northern
Ireland. The dilemma of identity imposed on the poet by the imprecise
status of this region is documented again in 'Singing School'. In 'The
Ministry of Fear' he explains the gradual moulding of his separate
Catholic/nationalist consciousness. At school he was told that Catholics
and Protestants can be distinguished by their accents and later he
discovers that his name too is a political label. Ultimately he confirms
one right that he knows is his, his entitlement to a place in the tradition
of English literature:

Ulster was British but with no rights on
The English lyric . . .

The strange phrases of his friend's poetry remain a mystery to the
enquiring police.

An instinctive sense of guilt is instilled in him at a young age and, in
'A Constable Calls', he fears the retribution that will be brought upon
his father for not registering the row of turnips in the constable's
record of local crops. A different sort of guilt overtakes him in 'Exposure'.
Having left the North of Ireland he finds that he is defending
himself against those who criticise him for not having adopted the role
of spokesman for the nationalist cause in his homeland.

The poems in which he does attempt to confront the brutal complexity
of the conflict in the North of Ireland refer back to the tribal precedents
of Germanic society. In 'Funeral Rites' he bemoans the lack of a
ritual that would bring meaning and coherence to the random deaths in
his society. His final image is taken from an Icelandic source, *Njal's
Saga*. Despite not having been avenged according to the traditional
code of honour, the pagan hero Gunnar was beautiful in death.

The acts of revenge carried out in the poet's society are alluded to in
'Punishment'. Here the Iron Age body of the young adulteress, described
in P.V. Glob's study *The Bog People*, is compared to those of
Belfast girls tarred and feathered for consorting with English soldiers.
The poet recognises in this act the survival of an ancient motive that
inspired Iron Age people in Northern Europe and in Northern Ireland.
He says that he would:

. . . connive
in civilised outrage
yet understand the exact
and tribal, intimate revenge.

In 'Kinship' too he is caught by the same double allegiance, worshipping a goddess no longer acknowledged in his society. Finally, he calls in Tacitus, the Roman historian of the Germanic tribes. The poet asks him to observe with detachment as his people kill each other in the name of self-protection.

The poet abdicates to the historian. He cannot view his own society with the necessary objectivity. His ritual southward progress in 'Funeral Rites' serves as a foreshadowing of the journey accomplished in 'Exposure'. The triumphal 'procession' becomes an isolated exile. The poet is, in the end, alone with his art.

For Heaney the north represents his home and this home by its name and location is associated with the bog. In 'Kinship' Seamus Heaney equates this native landscape with his own creative consciousness. It is at once 'outback of my mind' and 'vowel of earth'. This connection resonates through the poems in *North*. For him, ultimately, 'north' represents a country of the imagination. The cultural, historical, and political terrain uncovered in these poems is his own genetic map. It is the place where he grew up, the place where his attitudes and beliefs were formed; and, like the willow tree, his poetic imagination leans back into this place. Although in 'Exposure' he has moved south the season there is autumn as it was in 'Kinship'. From this perspective now he looks inward to himself and back towards the north.

---

(10) Choose two of the following topics and describe Seamus Heaney's treatment of them on the basis of his *Selected Poems 1965– 1975* : (a) love; (b) death; (c) faith; (d) fear.

OUTLINE:
(a) love: marital: 'Summer Home': dispute and resolution
             maternal: 'Mossbawn 1. Sunlight': foetus in womb:
             atmosphere
     Final images: definition of love

(b) death: metaphorical: 'Death of a Naturalist': child's physical
              innocence: fear
              actual: 'Funeral Rites': perfection of bodies by ritual:
              contrast: those killed by violence: alternative ritual:
              Gunnar.
     Both deaths: initiation process: revenge

ANSWER:
(a) *Love.* Two kinds of love have their place in the poems of Seamus Heaney, the romantic affection of a husband for his wife and the placid love of a mother for her child. In 'Summer Home' and 'Mossbawn: Sunlight' the poet expresses these through the evocation of a particular atmosphere and concludes with a definition of love.

Something has disturbed the love between the husband and wife in 'Summer Home'. He sets out to find the source of this tension, looking first outside themselves and outside their home. When he finds some insects hatching under the doormat he exterminates them. The dispute between the couple is not resolved by this action. The successive parts of the poem depict the poet and his wife being forced in upon themselves to find the cause of their discord, and to rediscover their love for one another.

Further attempts by the husband to appease his wife's self-pity fail. The armful of flowers he brings her fall between them, their love-making becomes aggressive and shocks them both. Finally they withdraw into themselves:

we sap
the white, trodden
path to the heart.

They wake in the morning to find the sun shining into their room, and the pain of their anger is soothed.

The poet's attitude to his wife is almost one of idolatry. In the second part of the poem his flowers are compared to a 'may altar' (a traditional household altar in honour of the Virgin Mary). With their perfume he would make a 'chrism' to 'anoint' the troubled area, a gesture that alludes to the ceremony of Blessing the Sick. After their love-making he watches his wife in the shower where her breasts, running with water, appear to him like 'stoups', receptacles for holy water found in a church. Their reconciliation comes with the solemnity of a ritual when 'dawn/Attends the pillow' and the light casts the vine and maize into relief like shadows of the wine and bread in a Catholic mass.

The cause of the dispute lies in the poet himself. His vehement action in the first verse betrays his guilt. It is as if by scalding the step he will purge himself. Hearing his wife sob and say his name he admits 'O love, here is the blame.' His anger drains them both and they are divided like the logs being split in Part IV, and in the next part he abuses her. His loudness is counterpointed by the small sound of love which they heard in the old cave. It resonates like the stalactite they knocked: 'Our love calls tiny as a tuning fork.' Against this precise sound the harmony of their love must be measured.

A similarly small image closes the first of the 'Mossbawn' poems. The poet has explained that 'Sunlight' is intended to be a description of the experience of a foetus in the womb. The woman to whom the poem is dedicated is his aunt.

The poet builds an atmosphere of warmth and patience through the selection of details revealing the empty calm of the yard and the easy movements of the woman baking. The pump, the bucket and the water in the yard, all are heated by the sun and, reflecting the light, the water takes on the appearance of honey.

Inside the kitchen the woman kneads the dough. Her preparation finished, she sits and waits by the oven for the scones to bake. The only sound to be heard is the 'tick of two clocks'. The warmth generated within the kitchen matches that of the sunlight outdoors and the poem moves inwards to a concentrated focus on the activity of the woman.

The emptiness of the place, the 'absence' in the yard, the 'space' in the kitchen are filled by this warmth and the attentive care of the woman's work, reproducing the expectant calm of a pregnancy. Beyond the probing light of the sun is the real source of this tranquillity:

> And here is love
> like a tinsmith's scoop
> sunk past its gleam
> in the meal-bin.

The work-worn implement mirrors the homely plainness of the woman whose fingernails are whitened by work, and whose legs are mottled by years of standing close to the heat of the oven.

The romantic love of husband and wife, and the patient love of the mother, are alike in their simplicity and endurance. Like the tin and the tuning fork love is to be found in small things and remains out of sight.

(b) *Death*. Seamus Heaney's first collection takes its title from the poem 'Death of a Naturalist'. The death in this poem is a metaphorical one; its title is a mildly ironic glance at the poet's early delight in the soft consistency of frogspawn and in the hatching tadpoles, and his subsequent fear of the frogs. Later, in 'Funeral Rites', he discusses the soothing effect that ritual has on actual death.

In the first of these poems the world is perceived through the sensibility of a young boy. Below the dam where the flax rots, and fills the air with its stench, the boy goes in search of frogspawn. This he brings home, delighted by the prospect of watching its small bubbles sprout into tadpoles. At school he is taught that the frogspawn is in fact the offspring of the frogs. This knowledge stays with him and when he returns to the dam and finds it occupied by frogs he panics at the thought that they will wreak revenge on him for stealing their young.

This sudden reversal of his feelings corresponds in one sense to the death of the boy's innocence. He had existed in a state of oblivious ignorance. The rotting flax was like a disease, 'festering' at the centre of the town, but this was obscured for the boy by the noise of the water and the colourful insects:

> Bubbles gargled delicately, bluebottles
> Wove a strong gauze of sound around the smell

He did not enquire into the nature of the frogspawn. The teacher addresses the class in a condescending tone and equates the parent frogs with the children's parents, calling them a 'Mammy' and a 'Daddy'. She tells them, too, about the croaking call of the frogs.

This simplistic information poisons the boy's pleasure and the gentle sounds of the first part of the poem are replaced by the loud croaking of the frogs, a sound like 'farting', and by the 'slap and plop' of their movements. All of these pose 'obscene threats' to the boy. The frogs seem to him as powerful as kings and as volatile as 'grenades'. Frightened and repulsed he runs away. His physical innocence is replaced by physical fear, a shift that carries implications of the beginning of a sexual awareness.

Funerals were also a form of initiation for young men. To carry a coffin was a mark of adult maturity. This is the scene with which 'Funeral Rites' opens. The ritual of the wake before the funeral was essential to the community's assimilation of the fact of death and provided a channel for their grief. The bodies, washed and laid out, attained a statuesque beauty, their faces like 'soapstone masks'. The poet and his family prayed before them, almost revering their death.

By contrast, in the second part of the poem, the poet laments the absence of any ritual that would absorb the shock and grief provoked by the frequent sectarian murders within his society. He tries to imagine a process that would provide the same solace as the traditional Christian one. The best he can propose is a procession to an ancient pagan site in the centre of Ireland. The masculine character of the ritual described in the first part which was an initiation into 'manhood', is even more pronounced in this ceremony, as the women are excluded and left in their homes to envisage the advance of the funeral towards the neolithic mounds beside the Boyne.

The communal necessity of the ritual is emphasised by the poet's description of the sectarian killings as 'each neighbourly murder'. The paradox of that expression reveals the disintegration of his society. Neighbour is killed by neighbour and every home is affected. The progress he depicts will have dignity, with the slow movement of cars and the beat of drums, but it will be sinister too:

Quiet as a serpent
in its grassy boulevard.

This is an image that reinforces its pagan aspect, a mode of belief banished from Ireland with the snakes.

The ritual is accomplished through the image of the Old Norse hero Gunnar. His perfection in death mirrors that of the poet's relatives in the first part and is the state that he hopes the murdered bodies will achieve. Gunnar was seen sitting upright in his burial mound singing the glory of honour even though his own death had not been honoured by revenge.

Both the figurative death of the young boy and the actual deaths in the poet's community are completed by images of vengeance. The child shares that perception of natural balance with the members of an ancient society. The menacing aspect of the frogs is matched by the menacing approach of the serpent. Unnatural death demands retribution. The stealing of the frogs' eggs and the murder of the poet's neighbours upset the equilibrium of life, and, in the primitive view, this can only be restored by a similar act. Ritual can glamorise a natural death but it will not resolve an untimely one.

---

(12) Compare the function and effect of the female voices in 'Undine' and 'The Wife's Tale'.

OUTLINE:
Function—poet: persona/mask: varies self-expression
               woman and fertility
               perspective on men
               contrast between male and female sensibility
Effect—   dramatic: poet playing a role
           anecdotal: myth/'tale'
           choice of images

Comparison of the two: both excluded from the labour; both connected with agriculture.

Contrast: the undine: semi-mythical; admitted into human life. The wife: silent, submissive, threatened.

ANSWER:
Both 'Undine' and 'The Wife's Tale' are concerned with the area of organic energy that is central to so many of Heaney's poems. Despite this significance both of these female personae are excluded from communal activity.

The undine speaks through her medium of water. Released from clogged drains by the farmer's spade, her delight is expressed in a seductive abandon:

    He halted, saw me finally disrobed,
    Running clear, with apparent unconcern.

As the farmer channels her into his fields she floods their soil, nourishing his crops. By this action the undine is united with him and becomes human.

Similarly, the wife in 'The Wife's Tale' is controlled by her husband. She cuts the bread as he likes it, and goes, at his insistence, to feel the seed he has just threshed. The frivolous pleasure of the undine is absent here and the wife is silent.

Adopting the role of these women the poet equips himself with a fresh perspective on the world. The actions of the men are calculated and aggressive. The words 'slashed' and 'shovelled' in the opening line of 'Undine' have a harsh sound contrasting with the light gurgle of the water. The wife sees the thresher operated by the men as something monstrous, its sound a 'hum and gulp', and its chute like 'jaws'.

Unlike the men, the women respond to their environment through their senses before their intellect. The undine feels her way through the soil and into the grain, eventually insinuating herself into the farmer's arms. The wife, when she examines the seed, contents herself with feeling it, weighing it in her hand, and confesses that she does not know what else to do with it. The title of this poem summarises the dismissive attitude of the farmer to his wife, an 'old wives' tale' being a popular expression applied to an unfounded superstition. In this spirit the farmer mocks his wife, joking about her elaborate preparation of the white cloth in the field, and lets her go when he and the men have finished eating. Her usefulness is finished.

The control of these women by the men alludes to their traditional repression. The undine in choked drains had been denied her 'right of way', the wife's silence is a brooding one. Dark forces menace her, like the monstrous machine; the seed feels to her like 'shot' and the pitch-forks standing upright in the ground resemble spears on a battlefield. This incongruous image reflects the archaic consciousness that the wife and the undine represent. Both poems are little fictions illustrating this awareness. 'Undine', according to the poet, developed out of the sound of the word, and his later discovery of the ancient tale of the undine's metamorphosis from water sprite to human. It is, he says, the archetypal myth of agriculture, the marriage of the farmer to his land. Conversely, the man in 'The Wife's Tale' sits back 'as proud as if he were the land itself', an image that is ironic in the context of the traditional association of the woman and the earth. Without admitting it, the husband depends on his wife to provide for him and to confirm his confidence in his harvest. The subservient silence of the wife is a metaphor for the subjection of women.

In the same way the sensual perception represented by these women is accorded less respect than the intellect. These characters, therefore, as they are depicted by the poet, are speaking from an area of his sensibility that is denied the right to expression. These are not real women, but idealised figures personifying this repressed area of consciousness. Their association with organic forces makes them, too, voices of that mysterious creative darkness which the poet is exploring through the collection *Door into the Dark*.

Part 5

Suggestions for further reading

The text

HEANEY, SEAMUS: *Selected Poems 1965–1975*, Faber and Faber, London, 1980. This is the text on which these notes are based.

Prose

HEANEY, SEAMUS: *Preoccupations: Selected Prose 1968–1978*, Faber and Faber, London, 1980.

Interviews

DRUCE, ROBERT: 'A Raindrop on a Thorn', *Dutch Quarterly Review*, 9, 1979, 24–37.
HAFFENDEN, JOHN: *Viewpoints: Poets in Conversation*, Faber and Faber, London, 1981, pp.57–75.

Criticism

CURTIS, TONY (ED.): *The Art of Seamus Heaney*, Poetry Wales Press, Cardiff, 1982. An uneven but generally useful series of essays by various critics including Philip Hobsbaum, one of the first people to encourage Seamus Heaney in his writing.
KING, P.R.: 'I Step through Origins: the Poetry of Seamus Heaney', *Nine Contemporary Poets: A Critical Introduction*, Methuen, London, 1979, Chapter 6, pp.191–218. This essay concentrates on the organic aspect of Seamus Heaney's early poetry.
MORRISON, BLAKE: *Seamus Heaney* (Contemporary Writers Series), Methuen, London and New York, 1982. This text is most helpful for the description it gives of the background to Seamus Heaney's work. The sources for many of the allusions contained in his poems are traced too. A good bibliography is included.

The author of these notes

AISLING MAGUIRE was educated at University College, Dublin, where she read English Language and Literature; in 1984 she completed a PhD thesis on the work of Seamus Heaney and Ted Hughes. She is at present teaching adults as part of a Community University Project in Dublin.